Preface Books

A series of scholarly and critical studies of major writers intended for those needing modern and authoritative guidance through the characteristic difficulties of their work to reach an intelligent understanding and enjoyment of it.

General Editor: JOHN PURKIS
Founding Editor: MAURICE HUSSEY

Portrait of Wilfred Owen, June 1916
Reproduced by permission of the Trustees of the Owen Estate

A Preface to Wilfred Owen

John Purkis

LONGMAN
London and New York

Addison Wesley Longman Limited
Edinburgh Gate
Harlow
Essex CM20 2JE
United Kingdom
and Associated Companies throughout the world.

*Published in the United States of America
by Addison Wesley Longman Inc., New York*

© Addison Wesley Longman Limited 1999

First published 1999

ISBN 0-582-27652-7   PPR
ISBN 0-582-27651-9   CSD

Visit Addison Wesley Longman on the world wide web at http://www.awl-he.com

British Library Cataloguing-in-Publication Data

A catalogue record for this book is available from the British Library

Library of Congress Cataloging-in-Publication Data

A catalog record for this book is available from the Library of Congress, USA

Set by 35 in $10\frac{1}{2}$/11pt Mono Baskerville
Produced by Addison Wesley Longman Singapore (Pte) Ltd.,
Printed in Singapore

Contents

List of illustrations

Acknowledgements

I should like to thank the editors and commentators upon Owen's poems who have enabled all of us to approach them as an open book; they had to come to terms with a series of texts which at one level communicate lucidly, but have often had to be freed from formidable difficulties. My debts are indicated in the Further Reading section of this book. I should also like to thank all who have helped me in the course of writing this book; in particular my Open University colleagues, Chris Emlyn-Jones, Lorna Hardwick, Tony Coe and Mags Noble, for making me clarify what I had to say about Owen; my wife Sallie for help with questions of historical context, and support during the process of composition. In conclusion I should salute the memory of my mother, Lilian Mary Comber, who served for four years as a member of the Women's Auxiliary Army Corps; like all of them, she never spoke of what she had seen, but it is just possible that at some point in the Great War she gave Wilfred Owen his tea.

Abbreviations

CL = *Wilfred Owen: Collected Letters*, ed. Harold Owen and John Bell (London, New York and Toronto: Oxford University Press, 1967)

Hibberd = Dominic Hibberd, *Wilfred Owen: The Last Year* (London: Constable, 1992)

JFO = Harold Owen, *Journey from Obscurity*, 3 vols (Oxford: Oxford University Press, 1963–65)

JS = Jon Stallworthy, *Wilfred Owen: A Biography* (London: Chatto/ Oxford University Press, 1974)

Kerr = Douglas Kerr, *Wilfred Owen's Voices: Language and Community* (Oxford: Clarendon Press, 1993)

Silkin = *The War Poems: Wilfred Owen*, ed. Jon Silkin (London: Sinclair-Stevenson, 1994)

Welland = D.S.R. Welland, *Wilfred Owen: A Critical Study* (London: Chatto and Windus, 1960)

Introduction

> When I go from hence let this be my parting word, that what I
> have seen is unsurpassable.
>
> Rabindranath Tagore, *Gitanjali*

These words were quoted by Wilfred Owen on several occasions,
and must refer to the quality and nature of his experiences during
the First World War of 1914–18. Whether those experiences were
'unsurpassable' must have given all readers of Owen cause for
thought, as the twentieth century has rolled by, piling horror upon
horror. Tied in with this idea is another point for discussion which is
still impossible to resolve adequately, though over a hundred years
have now gone by since the poet's birth: how far is Owen our contemporary? How far is he now a subject for historical study?

The memorial at Poets' Corner in Westminster Abbey firmly places
Owen in the context of his generation, those who suffered the horror of the First World War, or, as they referred to it, the Great War.
I have therefore tried to include as many references to other people's
experiences as I reasonably could, because a book that only referred
to Owen would be misleading; in particular we need to understand
how Owen fits into the poetic debate about the meaning of the war,
a debate started by Brooke, and challenged by Sorley, Graves and
Sassoon. On the other hand this is not a general study of First World
War poetry; in the final analysis the desire to write about Owen
singly and *as a poet* remains the overriding aim.

Such, however, is the dominance of Owen's poetry in the education of our sensibilities that he may be said to have established a
norm for the concept of 'war poetry' and permanently coloured the
view of the Great War for later generations. There is a need to
debate to what extent Owen's moral and emotional reaction to his
war experience was typical – or admirable. Every year more and
more books about the war display a myriad of quotations from
eyewitnesses which may be used for or against his viewpoint. A
recent book described the First World War as 'jolly'; while it is
certainly true that the war might have brought a few years of 'leave'
from a dull civilian job, it seems the final contradiction of Owen's
view to compare the Western Front to a holiday camp. Of course
the soldiers made themselves happy when they could and edited out
'gloom', but the hell was still there as the true reality. Indeed, hover-
ing over both Owen and other perceptive and truthful witnesses is a
compelling sense of the breaking of a taboo; it has to be borne in

mind that many survivors of the war never spoke of it subsequently. Their experiences were, in all senses of the word, 'indescribable'.

Verifying Owen's experience directly is not really the problem for the new reader of the 1990s and the twenty-first century. Because Owen was always a living poet to each subsequent generation – in the sense that he has never been relegated to a purely historical role in our consciousness – each generation has in turn modified what it has heard Owen saying and substituted what it has wanted him to say. For Sassoon in 1917 Owen was at first a disciple and a supporter in the public debate he was engaged in about the direction of the war; to Blunden in 1931 Owen was a victim of the war and also a poet who carried on the Romantic tradition of Keats and Shelley. But the readers of their editions soon had their own problems in the 1930s. Was not Owen a worthy ancestor of the peace movement? Then, as the Second World War came to an end, new horrors were revealed; the departure of the trains to the death-camps gave an additional layer of meaning to Owen's poem 'The Send-Off'. After the United Nations was founded, warfare was expected to keep its distance as a way of settling international conflicts; yet the 1950s saw first the Korean War – said to resemble the Great War in its conduct – and in 1956 the popular reaction against Eden's war in Suez. Owen may by then have seemed very much in the background but his massive influence in school education certainly dates from this period. In the mid-1960s the fiftieth anniversary of the Great War led to the celebratory-ironical scamper through *Oh What a Lovely War!*, though in Vietnam a different kind of hell was opened with photographers rather than poets seeming to inculcate Owen's values. Finally, and things are more difficult to evaluate as we come towards the present, the 1980s seemed to show Owen ignored: the Falklands War was an example of surprise at the bloody nature of conflict, which seemed to have been meant as an exercise in nostalgic glory. The Argentines were for years unforgiven; the example of reconciliation with the Germans which Owen and his contemporaries preached forgotten. Meanwhile the Iran/Iraq war with prolonged trench warfare over scraps of land, and the savagery of the Bosnian conflict, showed that a limited technology is no gentler than a full use of the powers of destruction now available. The final irony was the return of Sarajevo to the news – the very city which had ignited the First World War. All one asks is that readers should be aware of their own historical position before making judgements.

And so we return to the historical conundrum. How much is Wilfred Owen part of our present? As one sees the very last veterans of the Great War being paraded at Remembrance Day services, it is still possible to imagine that Owen might have survived into our own times. Other little details keep that war in our consciousness:

the popularity – if that is the right word – of school trips to the battlefields, the move to bring back the celebration of Remembrance once again to the 11 November at 11 a.m., and finally the unhealed wound in the psyche of our culture. Recent novels have underlined this strange contemporaneity.

In the second half of this book I have tried to show how Owen's very literary stance was formed by a limited number of earlier and contemporary influences; and secondly, to comment in detail upon some of his works which are exhibited in the order in which they were made available to the public. As in all Preface Books, the concluding section includes biographies of contemporaries and a Gazetteer; those who can visit Shropshire and make the pilgrimage to the grave at Ors will experience the shock of contrast between the two poles of Owen's existence, and perhaps understand the secret meaning of that parenthesis in one of Owen's last poems, 'Smile, Smile, Smile':

> (This is the thing they know and never speak,
> That England one by one had fled to France,
> Not many elsewhere now, save under France.)

Kate's Book

Part One
The Writer and His Setting

Chronology

	EVENTS IN WILFRED OWEN'S LIFE	EVENTS IN CULTURAL AND MILITARY HISTORY
1893	*18 March* Wilfred Owen born at Plas Wilmot, Shropshire.	
1895	Mary born.	H.G. Wells, *The Time Machine.*
1897	Harold born. Family move to Shrewsbury, then to Birkenhead.	
1899		Boer War begins.
1900	Colin born.	Oscar Wilde dies. John Ruskin dies. First Zeppelin flies.
1901	*11 June* WO enters Birkenhead Institute.	Queen Victoria dies. End of Boer War.
1902		Arnold Bennett, *Anna of the Five Towns.*
1904		France and Britain resolve differences. Russo-Japanese War.
1906		Liberal landslide victory in general election. HMS *Dreadnought* launched.
1907	Family returns to Shrewsbury. WO attends Shrewsbury Technical School.	Kipling wins Nobel Prize. Boy Scouts founded by Baden-Powell.
1908	*June* Holiday in Brittany with father.	Territorial Army formed. Asquith becomes Prime Minister.
1909	*July* Holiday in Brittany, then to Torquay.	Old Age Pensions are introduced. Swinburne dies.
1910		Two general elections – hung Parliament. Edward VII dies; George V succeeds to throne. Tolstoy dies.

EVENTS IN WILFRED OWEN'S LIFE	EVENTS IN CULTURAL AND MILITARY HISTORY
1911 *April* Visits Teignmouth while reading Keats's life. *Summer term* Works as pupil-teacher at Wyle Cop School, Shrewsbury. *September* Matriculates at London University. *20 October* Begins work at Dunsden, Oxfordshire, as pupil and assistant to Reverend Herbert Wigan.	
1912 At Dunsden. Makes approach to attend University College, Reading.	First *Georgian Poetry* anthology. *Titanic* disaster. Balkan Wars begin.
1913 *7 February* Leaves Dunsden. Ill for several months. *Summer* Sits for University College, Reading, scholarship but fails. *September* Begins work as English teacher at the Berlitz School, Bordeaux.	*Rite of Spring* ballet produced. D.H. Lawrence, *Sons and Lovers*.
1914	*28 June* Assassination of Archduke Franz Ferdinand in Sarajevo.
25 July Leaves Berlitz. Takes post as tutor with Léger family in the Pyrenees.	
	4 August Britain declares war on Germany. French government moved to Bordeaux. *31 August* Battle of Mons.
17 September Back in Bordeaux looking for freelance work.	
	9 October Fall of Antwerp.
8 December Begins working as tutor to the de la Touche boys at Mérignac.	
	16 December Scarborough shelled. *25 December* Christmas truce.

EVENTS IN WILFRED OWEN'S LIFE	EVENTS IN CULTURAL AND MILITARY HISTORY
1915	*January* First Zeppelin raids. *22 April* Gas first used at Ypres. *26 April* Allies land at Gallipoli. *May* Coalition government under Asquith.
May Goes to England for a holiday. *13 June* Returns to Bordeaux. *14 September* Escorts the de la Touche boys to England. Goes home to Shrewsbury.	*25 September* Battle of Loos begins. *12 October* Edith Cavell shot.
21 October Joins the Artists' Rifles. Lives in lodgings in London; meets Harold Monro at the Poetry Bookshop. *15 November* Training begins at Hare Hall Camp, Gidea Park.	
1916	*20 December* Gallipoli campaign abandoned. *February* Battle of Verdun begins. Easter Rising in Dublin.
4 June Receives commission in the Manchester Regiment. Attends further training courses for remainder of year.	*1 July* Battle of the Somme begins. *September* Tanks first used. *December* Lloyd George becomes Prime Minister.
30 December Posted to Étaples base camp, France.	

EVENTS IN WILFRED OWEN'S LIFE	EVENTS IN CULTURAL AND MILITARY HISTORY
1917 *1–2 January* Joins 2nd Manchester Regiment near Beaumont Hamel. *11 March* Bad fall into cellar. Concussed. *17 March* Sent to 13th Casualty Clearing Station.	
	2 April US enters the war.
4 April Returns to duty. Takes part in advance on St Quentin.	
	April Battle of Arras.
2 May Shell-shock. Sent to 13th Casualty Clearing Station. *11 June* Reaches No. 1 General Hospital, Étretat. *mid-June* Sent to Southampton, then to Welsh Hospital, Netley. *26 June* Arrives at Craiglockhart War Hospital, Edinburgh. *July* Becomes editor of *The Hydra* (hospital magazine).	
	31 July Third Battle of Ypres begins.
August Meets Siegfried Sassoon. *1 September* His first published poem – 'Song of Songs' – appears in *The Hydra*. *13 October* Introduced to Robert Graves.	
	25 October Revolution in Russia. Lenin takes over and sues for peace.
November Discharged and sent on leave. Meets London literati. *24 November* Takes up light duties with 5th Manchesters at	

EVENTS IN WILFRED OWEN'S LIFE	EVENTS IN CULTURAL AND MILITARY HISTORY
1918 Northern Cavalry Barracks, Scarborough. *23 January* Attends Robert Graves's wedding at St James's, Piccadilly. Meets Edward Marsh and C.K. Scott Moncrieff. *26 January* 'Miners' published in *The Nation*.	
	March German offensive and breakthrough in France.
12 March Posted to Northern Command Depot, Ripon. *4 June* Graded fit for service. *5 June* Rejoins the Manchesters at Scarborough. *15 June* 'Futility' and 'Hospital Barge at Cerisy' published in *The Nation*.	
	31 July German offensive crumbles. *8 August* Black day of the German Army.
31 August Returns to France.	
	September Germans in retreat.
1/2 October Awarded Military Cross.	
	31 October Peace overtures from the Central Powers.
4 November Killed in battle at the crossing of the Oise-Sambre canal.	
	11 November Armistice.
His mother receives the news of his death. He is buried in the village cemetery at Ors. 1919 Various poems published in magazines and in *Wheels*, the Sitwell anthology.	

7

EVENTS IN WILFRED OWEN'S LIFE	EVENTS IN CULTURAL AND MILITARY HISTORY
1920 *Poems*, includes twenty-three poems.	
1921 *Poems* reprinted with additional poem, 'The End'.	

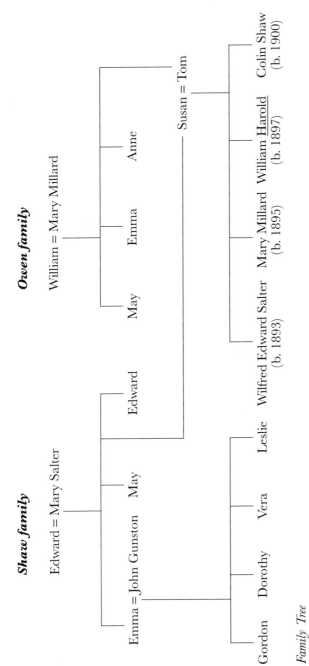

Family Tree

Shaw family

Edward = Mary Salter

Emma = John Gunston   May   Edward

Gordon   Dorothy   Vera   Leslie

Owen family

William = Mary Millard

May   Emma   Anne

Susan = Tom

Wilfred Edward Salter (b. 1893)   Mary Millard (b. 1895)   William Harold (b. 1897)   Colin Shaw (b. 1900)

1 Before battle: Owen's life prior to his enlistment in 1915

> Great-hearted son of Tydeus, why do you enquire about my family?
> The generations of men are just the same as the leaves.
> The wind showers one set of leaves to the ground, but the forest
> Produces others in abundance, as spring-time approaches.
> So with men: one generation grows up while another passes away.
> But if you really want to learn all about our family
> History: you'll find plenty of people who know it already.
>
> Homer, *Iliad* 6.145–51

Early life and education: 1893–1911

Wilfred Owen was born at Plas Wilmot, in the town of Oswestry in Shropshire, on 18 March 1893. Plas Wilmot was a six-bedroomed house of generous proportions which belonged to his maternal grandfather, Edward Shaw, and was temporarily the home of his parents, Tom and Susan Owen. They gave their first-born son the full name of Wilfred Edward Salter Owen, commemorating the ancestor who had built Plas Wilmot in the 1830s; in doing this they might also have been displaying aspirations to gentility. Tom Owen, who had begun life as a sailor and then became a railway clerk, might therefore have been thought to have married up, but this was not really the case. When Edward Shaw died in 1897, it became clear that the old man had lived beyond his means; the house had to be sold, and any delusions of grandeur came rapidly to an end.

Tom eventually found a better job with the Great Western Railway in Birkenhead, and after a series of moves[1] the Owens established themselves in a semi-detached house at 51 Milton Road. Wilfred was sent to the Preparatory School of the Birkenhead Institute in June 1899, moving up to the Junior School in 1901. In spite of the name, which might suggest either a state institution or a foundation similar to a Mechanics Institute, this was a fee-paying private school which one suspects the Owens could ill afford, but once again indicates the mother's aspirations for her first-born son.

By now there were three more children in the family – Mary, born 1895, Harold, born 1897, and Colin, born 1900. As they grew up they seem, in spite of the family's comparatively low income, to have striven to enjoy a 'respectable' middle-class family life, with visits to cousins and holidays by the sea; such escapes were made possible

by the occasional free rail travel which went with the father's oc-
cupation. The pattern of their life at Birkenhead continued until the
end of 1906 when Tom Owen was promoted to Assistant Superin-
tendent of the Joint Railways (i.e. the LNWR and GWR), necessit-
ating a move to Shrewsbury.[2] Though Wilfred wished to keep on at
the same school and board with a school friend, his mother insisted
that the whole family stayed together.

From early in 1907 Wilfred attended the Shrewsbury Technical
School; he was just coming up to fourteen, and doing well in French
and English. As time went on his letters to his cousins, the Gunstons,
show his interest in more scientific pursuits – Botany, Geology and
Astronomy. By 1909 this practical bent led him into exploring the
local archaeological site – Roman Uriconium, i.e. Wroxeter. In June
1910 the family moved to a house in Monkmoor Road, which Tom
Owen called 'Mahim' after a suburb of Bombay which he remembered from his travels; this house became their permanent home for
the rest of Wilfred's lifetime and beyond.

Wilfred's poetry will be discussed later, but it is important to note
that at this time – he was now seventeen – he had already begun to
write. His interest in the English Romantics had been encouraged at
school; this led him to attempt to write in the style of Keats. In 1911
he began to read Colvin's biography of the poet, and while on holiday at Teignmouth visited sites and houses associated with his hero.

Having now completed his school education, he worked as a pupil
teacher at Wyle Cop School in Shrewsbury while preparing for the
London Matriculation examination. To pass this was the essential
first step which would make possible entry to university and the
professions. But this would need money (see *CL* p. 76). He placed his
hopes upon getting a distinction in the exam, and perhaps then
obtaining a scholarship. In fact he passed the exam but without
achieving the distinction, and therefore decided to take up an offer
of parish work with the vicar of Dunsden, near Reading, who would
in return coach him for university entrance.

Before considering Owen's Dunsden experience it seems sensible
to reflect upon his education so far. In his own eyes he regarded
himself as a failure because of his results in the Matriculation examination. That Wilfred was bright there is no doubt, and speculation about how well he might have done at another type of school
or with other teachers is hardly useful. In fact, like many children
whose education leads them to enter a higher sphere than that of
their parents, Wilfred Owen did not know what to do at this point in
his life, and had no satisfactory role model or guidance. His parents
did not understand his capabilities; both in fact wanted quietly to
dominate their children's lives, to use their children to fulfil their
own fantasies. On the one hand his father, who had been to sea for

a short time and romanticised the experience, gave up on Wilfred and transferred his nautical ambitions to his second son Harold; on the other hand his mother's intense religiosity might well have influenced Wilfred, who was essentially a mother's boy, to try to please her by embarking on parish work for the Church of England. In this way he seems to have drifted into an area for which he was unprepared.

Dunsden: 1911–1913

On 11 October 1911 Owen took up his post as lay-assistant to the Reverend Herbert Wigan. In contrast to life in a suburb of Shrewsbury, the social arrangements of an English village must have seemed archaic; Wilfred Owen had a status thrust upon him which he had neither inherited nor earned. The new world which he entered had its own system of duties and obligations, fixed values and routines. Some were initially appealing: there was time to study and to write, and the vicarage had a full complement of servants to wait upon him. The vicar, a High Church Tractarian, now turned Evangelical, was dignified and aloof, but the general atmosphere of the vicarage seemed pleasant enough to Owen at first, and he liked his fellow-pupil, Alfred Saxby-Kemp. Parish work, on the other hand, meant contact with the inhabitants of rural slums; Wilfred therefore became, at various times, a teacher, a recorder of cases of extreme poverty, an inspector of insanitary accommodation, and a visitor of the sick: 'Consumption is all around us here. Scarlet Fever and Diphtheria are at work near by' (*CL* p. 109). One has to remember that there were no social services to speak of, though the Old Age Pension had just been introduced. Meanwhile, at least in its own heartland, the Church of England assumed responsibility for the souls and bodies of the rural poor.

There seems to have been very little in the way of the promised instruction from the vicar, but Owen was able to attend Botany classes at Reading University College from April 1912 and this led to an introduction to Miss Edith Morley, Head of English. She described him as an 'unhappy adolescent, suffering badly from lack of understanding . . . and in need of encouragement and praise' (*JS* p. 75). Her remarks provide one of the first independent assessments of Wilfred Owen, then aged nineteen. Undoubtedly the unhappiness was not helped by the pressures of religion.

While he seems to have been able to propagate the message of the Church, and to appear a believer in public, Owen's personal creed might well be described as 'Shelleyan'; this will be further explained when we look at poetic influences, but for the moment we are thinking of the revolutionary Shelley who despised priests and their systems of mental bondage. The antipathy of most nineteenth-century English writers to Evangelicalism's narrow creed is well documented, and Owen had absorbed these attitudes through his liberal education. He had already begun to mock the preaching at Dunsden in a letter to his mother (*CL* p. 120), and wrote again on 23 April that 'I am increasingly liberalising and liberating my thought, spite of the Vicar's strong Conservatism' (*CL* p. 131). A summer holiday with the family at Kelso relieved the situation, but it was followed by a week at an Evangelical Summer School at Keswick, which unleashed further troublesome reflections. In December the attempts of the vicar to stimulate a religious revival in the village seem to have precipitated a crisis.

By 4 January 1913 Wilfred was no longer able to maintain the balance between a very literal Bible-based Evangelicalism and Shelleyan 'atheism': the resolution, announced in the words 'I have murdered my false creed' (*CL* p. 175), shows that the victory lay with Shelley. On 7 February he left Dunsden, and spent the next month at home in a state of severe illness, described as 'congestion of the lungs'. Harold Owen felt that these physical symptoms 'came just in time to prevent a nervous breakdown' (*JFO* II p. 263), and added later: 'he had wasted those years as a mock-curate in Dunsden' (*JFO* III p. 44).

Looking ahead, it has been suggested that there seems to be some sort of pattern here – of psychological stress followed by breakdown – which may be seen as anticipating the shell-shock suffered on the Somme battlefield. In each case an initial period of enthusiasm is followed by a challenge to 'old' authority and perhaps an identification with the 'young' oppressed; certainly there is a compassion for the sufferings of the poor which greatly resembles his sympathy with the sufferings of the troops. Alternatively one could say that it is highly likely and hardly surprising that he had picked up an illness from his sick-visiting in the rural cottages; his mother thought he had caught tuberculosis.

Wilfred spent seven desultory months recovering from his illness. In April he was on holiday in Torquay, and again spent his time following up the references to Keats's poems and letters which the scenery provoked. In the summer he sat for a scholarship examination but failed to get into Reading University. This finally led him to follow up a plan which had been simmering in his mind for some time. He would go to France.

Bordeaux

Wilfred had long had an ambition to study in France for a year or two – originally after taking his degree (*CL* p. 76). In September

1913 he obtained a part-time teaching post at the Berlitz School in Bordeaux, of which his brother commented:

> The pay was pathetically small, and, under the system, precarious, and after working it out it seemed almost impossible that he could manage to live on it. But he was excited and keen to take it up; it was a chance to get to France, and the very nature of his work would be the best possible way to fulfil a minor ambition – to speak and think precisely as a French-born national. (*JFO* II p. 265)

It was also thought that his poor state of health would benefit from a winter in the south. The letters home from Bordeaux are much concerned with illness at first, but the regime of the Berlitz School must have been – in all senses – killing; he suffered from gastroenteritis and had to take time off from work. After Christmas things improved. He made friends with the parents of two of his pupils and enjoyed weekends in the country. In a letter to his mother of 24 May 1914 a long self-examination (in the Evangelical tradition) shows how much he thought he had grown in mental stature:

> When I ask myself *what* I am I finish my interrogations in a *crise de nerfs*. You see these self-examinations, after a year's rest, begin again. At such times the sensation of the passing of Time sharpens into agony. How much have I advanced in study since the Matriculation 1911? Enormously in some fields, but not along the marked-out high-roads, and through those absurd old toll-gates called examinations. (*CL* p. 254)

The letter concludes, after discussing the appeal of music and art, with a re-dedication to poetry.

Owen was uncertain what to do in the summer when regular teaching fell away; then he was invited by one of his pupils, Madame Léger, to accompany her family to Bagnères-de-Bigorre in the Pyrenees. It was the beginning of August 1914: though the onset of the war seems to have been unforeseen, in other senses all was prepared, even in the remotest villages of France. There was an instant mobilisation of all the young men, so that Wilfred wrote home on 8 August: 'Practically all the men have now gone to join their corps' (*CL* p. 272). Wilfred was noticeable as he looked French, and had to get a permit to remain. But he was excited by the outbreak of war and wrote to Colin on 10 August: 'I have almost a mania to be in the East, to see fighting, and to serve' (*CL* p. 274). These were the expected sentiments of the time, but even for that time it is a little unexpected to find the following 'eugenic' observations, saved only a little by the presence of irony:

I feel my own life all the more precious and more dear in the presence of this deflowering of Europe. While it is true that the guns will effect a little useful weeding, I am furious with chagrin to think that the Minds which were to have excelled the civilization of ten thousand years, are being annihilated – and bodies, the product of aeons of Natural Selection, melted down to pay for political statues. I regret the mortality of the English regulars less than that of the French, Belgian, or even Russian or German armies: because the former are all Tommy Atkins, poor fellows, while the continental armies are inclusive of the finest brains and temperaments of the land. (*CL* p. 282)

These views did not survive the sight of the first wounded, some of whom were being treated in a local hospital. It is also significant that in August he met the poet Laurent Tailhade, a former pacifist, who was to demonstrate his change of heart by enlisting at the age of fifty-nine.

Owen was obviously confused by the situation in Bordeaux. The Berlitz School had closed and so he thought seriously of returning to England, but there were problems about the permitted route for a start. He therefore looked around for pupils, and eventually found himself engaged as private tutor to the four de la Touche boys; these were English children who had been left stranded in France by the war. On 19 December 1914 he joined this family at Mérignac, just outside the town, with the proviso that he could continue to teach his other pupils in Bordeaux during the day.

By this time the war had become a settled-in phenomenon. Owen, like many others, had lost much of his initial interest in the progress of the conflict. He wrote to his mother in the new year: 'One thinks of the trenches with guilty feelings, in the midst of my surroundings . . .' (*CL* p. 311). He had intended perhaps to return home in January, but his commitment to the de la Touche boys had led him into a kind of trap, and it is too easy to say that he should have made up his mind to enlist. It was his obligations to this English family that led to the prolongation of his stay in France until almost the end of September 1915. The difficulties of obtaining a suitable and safe Channel crossing for himself and the boys were now exacerbated by submarine warfare. Even though he did return by himself to England for a month in May, he still went back again to France in order to escort the children across the Channel in September.

Once again some analysis is necessary before we continue the story. This French experience of almost two years – September 1913 to September 1915 – cries out for more assessment than it has so far received. It more or less coincided with the time and the age normally spent by a young person at a university. One might add that two years' almost continuous experience of listening to and speaking French, imbibing French life and culture, both in lodgings and in families, seems curiously underplayed in accounts of Wilfred Owen's life compared to the three to five months in France of early 1917 (two months of which were in hospital anyway) and the three months from August to November 1918. (I am deliberately ignoring the war situation and the trenches, but the Army was virtually an all-British environment anyway, so that Owen would be remarkable because he was able to converse with French people.) Of course Owen's war-time experiences were of a different intensity, but his civilian days in France were also formative. I feel that one needs to revalue the Frenchness of Owen's character, of his approach to life and morals, and of his poems. It is well observed that exposure to another language sharpens our feeling for our own.

Although his family were not satisfied with his choice of job as a language teacher, one must stress some positives. In the first place it was his own choice, not his mother's, and corresponds in a way with his father's independent and romantic gesture of serving 'before the mast'; it is significant that this frequently ignored father did visit him in Bordeaux. Secondly, it had the effect of reversing the judgements on his character which the Dunsden experience might have led us to make. There, you might say, he ran away; in this case he did stick at the job in spite of ill-health and the onset of war, factors which would have caused many others in the same situation to return home. He showed a sense of responsibility to others, particularly the de la Touche boys. He grew up.

Furthermore he occasionally spoke – in a way that seems quite out of character – of embarking on business-ventures; he had no wish to return to England and enter upon a conventional teaching career. He had been cautioned at an early stage to avoid toiling as an elementary schoolteacher (*CL* p. 70), but this kind of enterprise would not be the only alternative. Looking ahead for a moment, in March 1917 he was to tell Colin that after the war he had 'determined to keep pigs' (*CL* p. 446).

In contrast to the earlier abandonment of Evangelical Christian belief which had led to his departure from Dunsden, he developed an interest in the religious ceremonies of the Catholic Church. At first he frequented the Protestant Christian Union and reported dutifully to his mother on the quality of 'Religious Life' in Bordeaux, insisting that he was attending a Bible class (*CL* p. 227). At the same time, however, he told her that he had attended 'my first real, Catholic mass' (*CL* p. 224); this was followed by a funeral service (*CL* p. 248) and mass at Easter, which Stallworthy thinks may have been the origin of the poem 'Maundy Thursday'. Certainly his interest in these rituals and their language may also be seen to lie behind his later elegies.

17

Finally, and it is good to conclude on a cheerful note, his letters from this period reveal a curiously Keatsian sense of enjoying life's pleasures to the full in spite of the hard work, and he refers to Keats in a letter to Leslie Gunston of July 1915:

> I wonder that you don't ply me with this argument: that Keats remained absolutely indifferent to Waterloo and all that commotion. Well, I *have* passed a year of fine-contemptuous nonchalance: but having now some increase of physical strength I feel proportionately useful and proportionately lacking in sense if I don't use it in the best way – The Only Way. (*CL* p. 349)

For all his time in France Owen seems to have felt a sense of impending trial of strength; he thought that his choice was between the interview 'either with a Professor or a Recruiting Sergeant' (*CL* p. 305), but in fact only one road would be open to him.

Notes

1   See JS pp. 13ff., especially the quotations from *JFO*, to appreciate the details of lower-middle-class horror evoked by the industrial town.
2   His salary eventually rose to £200 a year *c.* 1914 (*JFO* III p. 106 n.). Of course the purchasing power of this sum was enough to secure a reasonably comfortable existence at the time.

2   *During the war*

'You know, Harold, if I have got to be a soldier, I must be a good one, anything else is unthinkable. I cannot alter myself inside nor yet conform but at least without any self-questioning I can change outside, if that is what is wanted.'

(JFO III p. 155)

Every subject's duty is the king's; but every subject's soul is his own.

Shakespeare, *Henry V* IV.1

Enlistment and training: 1915–1916

At this stage in the war the British Army was still recruited from volunteers. However, if Wilfred Owen had not joined up upon his return to England the social pressures on him to do so would have been very strong. Within the family – though evidence is lacking – his father was surely keen; his mother's views are not clear but she does not seem to have been opposed to his decision. An obscure poem, to be discussed later, called 'The Kind Ghosts' (see p. 121) has been interpreted as showing Owen's censure of a mother-figure quietly profiting from the death of her 'boys'; but as the word 'mother' does not occur in the poem it is a very far-fetched interpretation, and unlikely to be relevant.

After a month's holiday Wilfred went up to London and joined the Artists' Rifles; he had earlier discovered that this might be a quick route to a commission. He was sworn in on 21 October 1915 at the headquarters in Duke's Road. The fact that he lodged temporarily in 'a French Boarding House, where Guests, Conversation, Cooking, and everything else is French' (*CL* p. 359) was partly luck but also seems to represent a last wave to the experience of France. After this all his linguistic facility in French seems to have been forgotten in the rush of experience of Army life – one feels that some other organisation might have picked him out for special liaison duties with the French forces, but this didn't happen under the inflexible British Army system. For the next few months he was to receive basic training of the usual idiotic kind: 'We had to practise Salutes (on Trees) this very morning' (*CL* p. 362). Near him in Bloomsbury he discovered the Poetry Bookshop, an enterprise begun by Harold Monro, which also offered convenient lodgings; he began to plan a move there, but this idea was overtaken by events.

19

In November he left central London and was posted to Hare Hall, Gidea Park, Romford, Essex, to continue his training. This was now an Army camp and he was soon familiarised with the duties of military life. By the end of November he had moved up from Private to Cadet; he experienced guard duty (*CL* p. 367), and fatigues. There was no Christmas leave but he was able to get home for a few days in the New Year. He also saw his brother who was on leave from the merchant navy; Harold has left a vivid account of these meetings (*JFO* III 141–51).

In March 1916 Wilfred joined the Officers' School, which was also situated at Romford. He passed his exams and after leave in May was gazetted as Second Lieutenant on 4 June. From 18 June he began his duties as an officer of the 5th Battalion of the Manchester Regiment at Milford Camp, Witley, near Guildford. The remainder of the year was spent in further training courses at Aldershot, Oswestry and Southport. Owen was very proficient on the firing range, becoming a first class shot, and seems to have been retained by the commanding officer to assist in training others. He ended the year in charge of the Brigade Firing Point at Fleetwood. For these reasons he lost touch with most of his junior officer contemporaries, who had by now been posted to France. But after Christmas leave he too was sent on his way and found himself at Folkestone on 29 December.

Into battle

The New Year of 1917 was therefore spent in France. Wilfred arrived at the enormous base camp at Étaples and was immediately ordered to proceed forward to join the 2nd Manchesters who were 'resting' from a severe battle at Halloy, near Beaumont Hamel. Owen's journey to find them is described as being 'let down, gently, into the real thing, Mud'. He began to encounter the chaos which real war produces, and to experience the difference between training and the field of operations – 'The English seem to have fallen into the French unhappy-go-lucky non-system' (*CL* p. 422).

By 7 January the 2nd Manchesters had moved forward to Beauval and then to Bertrancourt – nearer and nearer to the front line. The keenness of the recently trained man is seen in the following episode:

> I chose to spend an hour today behind the guns (to get used to them). The Major commanding the Battery was very pleasant indeed. He took me to his H.Q. and gave me a book of Poems to read as if it were the natural thing to do!! But all night I shall be hearing the fellow's voice: Number Two – FIRE! (*CL* p. 425)

One inevitably calls to mind the words of a later poem, 'Insensibility': 'cursed are dullards whom no cannon stuns'. His letters home are also full of requests for necessaries which (though perfectly normal for the time) convey the atmosphere of a scout camp in the Lake District: ' I want a large, soft sleeping helmet and refills for the lamp' (*CL* p. 425). In appearance, he tells his mother, 'I am transformed now, wearing a steel helmet, buff jerkin of leather, rubber-waders up to the hips, & gauntlets. But for the rifle, we are exactly like Cromwellian Troopers' (*CL* p. 426).

On 12 January they moved into the line at Beaumont Hamel and found themselves in the closing stages of what had started out so optimistically as the Battle of the Somme. On 16 January he wrote to his mother: 'I have not been at the front. I have been in front of it.' The intensity of battle was palpably felt and vividly recounted; one can see in the letters the germs of later poems. 'I kept my own sentries half way down the stairs during the more terrific bombardment. In spite of this one lad was blown down and, I am afraid, blinded' (*CL* p. 428; see 'The Sentry', p. 109).

These experiences of heavy shelling and extreme danger took their toll of his fellow officers in the line; one, he reports, is 'completely prostrated and is in hospital'; another, who relieved him, is to be court-martialled for leaving '3 Lewis Guns behind when he came out'. One sees here Owen trying to please his father (see *CL* p. 431) as well as his mother with stories of his competence and bravery in his first action, while other parts of the letter — 'I nearly broke down', 'I am never going back to this awful post' – seem to hint at the nervous exhaustion to which all were prone, and which had begun to work even upon the new arrival on the battlefield.

After five days they retired to a ruined village, safe but extremely cold; after this period of rest the regiment then returned to the front line. This spell of duty lasted to the end of January when Owen was sent to Abbeville to attend a transport course for one month. Although the internal combustion engine had long been invented, most of the transport of the Great War involved the management of horses, and Owen was amazed to find that the course included 'circus tricks'. Owen became Mess President – an unlikely honour and also a chore, but it may be evidence of Wilfred's new sociability that Harold had also noticed while seeing him in training. In addition he found a little time to write poems. It is worth noting – in response to the popular view that the war poets wrote about their experiences immediately as if they were reporters – that Owen does not at this stage seem to have written about the war at all, but continued to devote his time to sonnets on 'Golden Hair' and other aesthetic subjects in competition with his cousin Leslie and Miss Joergens. The thought of these aesthetes carrying on a poetry correspondence course with Wilfred – who had just suffered the extremes of battle – has its own delicious ironies. It is also important to note that a poem with a hint of erotic misbehaviour was to be shown to his mother, but not to be taken literally: 'On the contrary I have been a very good boy . . .' (*CL* p. 437).

On 1 March he returned to the battalion and to the front line near Fresnoy: at first they were in dugouts at Bouchoir, slightly to the rear. Nearer the line itself they began to dig in, but this proved pointless because in fact the Germans were engaged in a phased withdrawal to the Hindenburg Line. The salient was proving too costly to hold and the German commanders were wisely moving back to positions which they had been able to construct at leisure, as it were; they would also shorten their front by 25 miles. Owen's period in the front line came to an abrupt end during the night of the 13/14 March when he fell down a hole into a well, and developed symptoms of delayed concussion.

By the 17th he had been moved back to a Casualty Clearing Station at Gailly: he was not considered to be too serious a case, and so was not moved further back from the line. In fact he had the leisure and the mental alertness to write 'Sonnet – with an Identity Disc' which was sent to his brother Colin on 24 March. He was kept at the Clearing Station until he was completely recovered, and had time to visit Amiens. He was discharged at the end of March.

When he eventually caught up with his battalion on 4 April, he found that they had made a considerable advance; after fierce fighting they had arrived at Selency on the outskirts of St Quentin. On 8 April Owen told his mother that he had survived an action in which several others had been wounded:

> We stuck to our line 4 days (and 4 nights) without relief, in the open, and in the snow. Not an hour passed without a shell amongst us. I never went off to sleep for those days, because the others were far more fagged after several days of fighting than I fresh from bed. We lay in wet snow. I kept alive on brandy, the fear of death and the glorious prospect of the cathedral Town just below us, glittering with the morning. (*CL* pp. 449–50)

This is one of several experiences that winter which may have contributed to the poem 'Exposure' (see p. 113).

He had expected that 8 April would have been the beginning of a long rest period, but almost immediately the battalion was ordered back to Savy to support the French, who intended to attack St Quentin. In the end they spent twelve days in the line and Owen underwent the unsettling experience which may have contributed to his illness: according to the received lore of the time, the explosion of a shell might produce the effects of 'shell-shock'.

I think the worst incident was one wet night when we lay up against a railway embankment. A big shell lit on the top of the bank, just 2 yards from my head. Before I awoke, I was blown in the air right away from the bank! I passed most of the following days in a railway Cutting, in a hole just big enough to lie in, and covered with corrugated iron. My brother officer of B Coy, 2/Lt Gaukroger lay opposite in a similar hole. But he was covered with earth, and no relief will ever relieve him, nor will his rest be a 9 days-Rest. (*CL* p. 452)

Here again we have an experience which may have contributed to the genesis of a poem (see the discussion of 'Strange Meeting', p. 101).

On 1 May – the battalion being then withdrawn for rest – Owen was noticeably unwell, and was sent back to hospital. At the time it might have been considered that such a nervous collapse – Owen says he was 'shaky' – savoured of cowardice, and there seems to be some evidence that his commanding officer was displeased for this reason. Owen told his mother that he was 'labelled Neurasthenia. I still of course suffer from the headaches traceable to my concussion . . . . Do not for a moment suppose I have had a "breakdown"' (*CL* p. 453). He seems at first to have been in good humour, and anxious to avoid any suggestion that he was a mental case. Some of his letters home are certainly strange, but there is some evidence of trench fever – with a high temperature – contributing to his state of mind.

After a variety of changes of scene spread over a long period, which seems to indicate that his general condition was worsening, he arrived at Étretat on 11 June and was then sent via Southampton to the Royal Victoria Hospital, then known as the Welsh Hospital, Netley. After nearly a fortnight's stay there he was examined by a Medical Board on 25 June. The conclusion was: 'There is little abnormality to be observed but he seems to be of a highly-strung temperament. He has slept well while here.' While this might seem to imply that his was not a serious case, the last remark surely refers to night-disturbances or indicates that he had suffered from bad dreams. This was a typical feature of 'shell-shock', and explains why he was considered to be unfit for service for the next six months; it was decided that he was to be transferred to Craiglockhart War Hospital, Edinburgh. His behaviour by day was obviously completely reasonable as he was allowed to proceed to Edinburgh unaccompanied.

Craiglockhart

Craiglockhart was a Hydro, or Hydropathic Establishment; that is it was built for the practice of the watercure, which had become unfashionable. It therefore gave every appearance of having seen better days. It now functioned as a military hospital for shell-shocked officers. The situation, atmosphere and treatment meted out at Craiglockhart have been well described by Siegfried Sassoon. The officers detained there were completely free by day, but night had its own special terrors:

> by night they [the doctors] lost control and the hospital became sepulchral and oppressive with saturations of war experience. One lay awake and listened to feet padding along passages which smelt of stale cigarette-smoke; for the nurses couldn't prevent insomnia-ridden officers from smoking half the night in their bedrooms, though the locks had been removed from all doors. One became conscious that the place was full of men whose slumbers were morbid and terrifying – men muttering uneasily or crying out in their sleep. . . . In the day-time, sitting in a sunny room, a man could discuss his psycho-neurotic symptoms with his doctor, who could diagnose phobias and conflicts and formulate them in scientific terminology. . . . But by night each man was back in his doomed sector of a horror-stricken front line where the panic and stampede of some ghastly experience was re-enacted among the livid faces of the dead. No doctor could save him then, when he became the lonely victim of his dream disasters and delusions.[1]

Whereas Sassoon was under the care of Dr W.H.R. Rivers, Owen was assigned to Captain Brock, who believed in the discipline of work and healthy open-air activities. Botanical excursions and swimming are mentioned by Wilfred. Poetry – on suitable themes – was also encouraged in Owen's case and he began a long poem on Hercules and Antaeus called 'The Wrestlers'; he also took on the editorship of *The Hydra – Journal of Craiglockhart War Hospital*. He was further employed in giving lectures on botanical subjects, engaged in amateur dramatics, and began to take a course in German. His mother came to see him, and, generally speaking, he was beginning to recover his old joy in life, though some of his letters still seem to be emotionally unbalanced.

The even tenor of his life was abruptly changed when he realised that Siegfried Sassoon had arrived at Craiglockhart: 'I have just been reading Siegfried Sassoon,[2] and am feeling at a very high pitch of emotion. . . . That is why I have not yet dared to go up to him and parley in a casual way' (*CL* pp. 484–5). But he did dare and soon began exchanging civilities and then poems for comment. The first of these – 'The Deadbeat' – was, as Owen said, 'in Sassoon's style', for Owen found himself drawn to imitate Sassoon's anti-war poems with their colloquial diction and sarcasm (see pp. 69–70). From August to November Owen met Sassoon nearly every evening. At first Owen received Sassoon's tuition, though later Sassoon began to wonder who had been teaching whom. For example, Sassoon's praise of 'Song of Songs' (see p. 84), with its consonantal rhyme-scheme, meant that Owen began to experiment with further possibilities of this new form of half-rhyme or assonance. The tuition culminated in the prolonged rewriting of the 'Anthem for Doomed Youth', at the end of which, Sassoon wrote later, he began to see:

> that my little friend was much more than the promising minor poet I had hitherto adjudged him to be. I now realized that his verse, with its sumptuous epithets and large-scale imagery, its noble naturalness and the depth of meaning, had impressive affinities with Keats, whom he took as his supreme exemplar. This new sonnet was a revelation . . .[3]

Throughout the autumn Wilfred improved in health, but still had some horrid nights and so was kept on at the hospital after the first period of rehabilitation was over. His friendship with Sassoon led to a new circle of acquaintants; he met another poet, Robert Graves, in October. When Owen finally left Craiglockhart in November Sassoon gave him an introduction to Robert Ross, the former friend of Oscar Wilde, who had become one of the leaders of literary life in London.

A period of leave followed his discharge. After a few days in Shrewsbury Owen found himself in London on 9 November, dining with Ross, H.G. Wells and Arnold Bennett at the Reform Club. In several letters he dwelt on this and other meetings with Ross's friends as an initiation into the higher ranks of literature, while seeing all the time the comic side of these examples of genius. He then invited Leslie Gunston to meet him in Winchester; a few days later he wrote a letter to him which can be read purely as a kind of metaphorical seeing : 'I could almost see the dead lying about in the hollows of the downs' (*CL* p. 508) – but could on the other hand indicate that he was still in a state in which he confused the dreams of night-time with the reality of day.

Scarborough, Ripon and return to the front

After three weeks' leave Owen reported to the reserve battalion of the Manchesters in Scarborough, and found himself in charge of a hotel where the officers were quartered; this was 'Light Duty' with a vengeance.

> I am Major Domo of the Hotel. . . . I have to control the Household, which consists of some dozen Batmen, 4 Mess Orderlies, 4 Buglers, the Cook, (a fat woman of great skill,) two female kitcheners, and various charwomen! (*CL* pp. 508–9)

Having mastered the situation, he found more time for writing poems, and by the New Year was able to sum up his life so far in a letter to his mother:

> Everything has been done in bouts:
> Bouts of awful labour at Shrewsbury & Bordeaux; bouts of amazing pleasure in the Pyrenees, and play at Craiglockhart; bouts of religion at Dunsden; bouts of horrible danger on the Somme; bouts of poetry always; of your affection always; of sympathy for the oppressed always.
>
> I go out of this year a Poet, my dear Mother, as which I did not enter it. I am held peer by the Georgians; I am a poet's poet. (*CL* p. 521)

In fact he now seems far more assured in his personal life, attending Robert Graves's wedding at St James's, Piccadilly, and behaving as if this was the life of the gentleman he was born to be.

In March he was transferred to the Depot at Ripon: this seemed tough at first:

> An awful Camp – huts – dirty blankets – in fact WAR once more. Farewell Books, Sonnets, Letters, friends, fires, oysters, antique-shops. Training again! (*CL* p. 538)

and so, in search of some privacy, he found himself a room outside camp in Borrage Lane. There he revised his poems. But the 'real war' in France had not ceased to haunt him, and now appeared to be moving towards crisis. As the great German offensive of March 1918 progressed he had a 'vision of the lands about St. Quentin crawling with wounded' (*CL* p. 544). He continued to keep up with his new London friends, visiting them in May, and finding enough encouragement to prepare a book of his poems for publication.

He returned to Scarborough in June and began the immense task of organising the feeding of the new recruits – by this time the war in France was demanding all available officers and men. As Owen's health improved he seems to have made up his mind to return to the front, but this may be based on misinterpretation of his letters. In any case he was not able to pass the Medical Board. By the end of August, however, he was fit enough to go, and the system would have demanded his presence in the front line. He arrived in Étaples on 1 September.

It took some time to find the battalion, which was halted in a rest area just east of Amiens. He finally rejoined them on 15 September, and was appointed Bombing Officer. The troops called him 'The Ghost', presumably because they were amazed at his return. They moved back to the line on 28/29 September and came under fire on the 30th at Magny-la-Fosse, north of St Quentin. A fierce fight developed during the next day as they moved forward into the German strongpoint. Owen tells his mother that in the exultation of battle

> I lost all my earthly faculties, and fought like an angel. . . .
> You will guess what has happened when I say I am now Commanding the Company. . . .
> I have been recommended for the Military Cross. . . .[4]
> My nerves are in perfect order. (*CL* p. 580)

It has been suggested that part of the bravado of this letter is a concealed message to his father, who had felt, it seems, that the earlier neurasthenia had been a cowardly excuse for avoiding the fighting. Certainly all this must have restored Wilfred's faith in himself, now that his courage as a soldier was confirmed.

The battalion moved forward in pursuit of the fleeing Germans, whose morale had now cracked. The Manchesters were ordered to attempt the crossing of the Sambre/Oise canal near Ors. They went into battle in the early morning of 4 November; but the German machine-guns dominated the action from the far bank of the canal. It was a fiercely contested crossing. Owen was killed while encouraging his men.

Notes

1   Siegfried Sassoon, *Sherston's Progress* (London: Faber and Faber, 1936), pp. 86–8.
2   In *The Old Huntsman and Other Poems* (London: William Heinemann, 1917).
3   Siegfried Sassoon, *Siegfried's Journey 1916–1920* (London: Faber and Faber, 1945), pp. 59–60.
4   The official citation is as follows: 'For conspicuous gallantry and devotion to duty in the attack on the Fonsomme Line on 1st/2nd October 1918. On the Company Commander becoming a casualty, he assumed command and showed fine leadership and resisted a heavy counter-attack. He personally captured an enemy Machine Gun in an isolated position and took a number of prisoners. Throughout he behaved most gallantly.'

3   Afterwards

Both books [Stallworthy's biography and Hibberd's *The Last Year*]
stop where Owen's life really begins – with his death.
                    Geoff Dyer, *The Missing of the Somme* (1995), p. 30

Family matters

Jon Stallworthy's biography of the poet concludes with three epis-
odes which must be mentioned here. First there was the supreme
irony for the Owen family, that the telegram announcing the death
of their son was delivered on 11 November 1918, just as the church
bells were ringing to celebrate victory. Though it is easy to curse
retrospectively the powers that be for the unnecessary waste of life in
the concluding stages of the war, when it seems that peace could
have been had for the asking, there were military considerations
which must have seemed paramount at the time. The enemy had if
possible to be driven out of the territory he had occupied, and in
particular out of his strongpoints in case the peace failed to hold. It
is also worth commenting, as we contemplate the manner of his
death, that in neither of his tours of duty at the front had Owen in
fact suffered the stalemate of 'trench warfare' which is usually identified as the typical experience of the Western Front. On both occasions he had taken part in the excitement of forward movement, and
the final stages of the war were 'the break-out' which had eluded the
British Army for so long. But obviously, in campaigns where any
advance was usually terminated by the use of the machine-gun, such
a war of movement would inevitably generate considerable casualties.
   A second incident which took place on Armistice Day cannot
really be discussed at all; I reprint without comment the following
episode from Harold Owen's autobiography:

> We were lying off Victoria. I had gone down to my cabin thinking
> to write some letters. I drew aside the door curtain and stepped
> inside and to my amazement I saw Wilfred sitting in my chair. I
> felt shock run through me with appalling force and with it I could
> feel the blood draining away from my face. I did not rush towards
> him but walked jerkily into the cabin – all my limbs stiff and slow
> to respond. I did not sit down but looking at him I spoke quietly:
> 'Wilfred, how did you get here?' He did not rise and I saw that he
> was involuntarily immobile, but his eyes which had never left mine
> were alive with the familiar look of trying to make me understand;

when I spoke his whole face broke into his sweetest and most endearing dark smile. I felt no fear – I had not when I first drew my door curtain and saw him there; only exquisite mental pleasure at thus beholding him. All I was conscious of was a sensation of enormous shock and profound astonishment that he should be here in my cabin. I spoke again. 'Wilfred dear, how can you be here, it's just not possible. . . .' But still he did not speak but only smiled his most gentle smile. This not speaking did not now as it had done at first seem strange or even unnatural; it was not only in some inexplicable way perfectly natural but radiated a quality which made his presence with me undeniably right and in no way out of the ordinary. I loved having him there: I could not, and did not want to try to understand how he had got there. I was content to accept him, that he was here with me was sufficient. I could not question anything, the meeting in itself was complete and strangely perfect. He was in uniform and I remember thinking how out of place the khaki looked amongst the cabin furnishings. With this thought I must have turned my eyes away from him; when I looked back my cabin chair was empty. . . .

I felt the blood run slowly back to my face and looseness into my limbs and with these an overpowering sense of emptiness and absolute loss. . . . I wondered if I had been dreaming but looking down I saw that I was still standing. Suddenly I felt terribly tired and moving to my bunk I lay down; instantly I went into a deep oblivious sleep. When I woke up I knew with absolute certainty that Wilfred was dead. (*JFO* III pp. 198–9, as quoted in JS p. 287)

Finally, there is the matter of Wilfred's grave and its inscription. His body was buried in the village cemetery at Ors, a far less intimidating setting than the vast military cemeteries which the Allies constructed in France after the war. Nevertheless, as in those cemeteries, the gravestones of the British soldiers were kept to one design; the only variation permitted to the families was a space for an inscription at the foot. There his mother placed a quotation from Owen's poem 'The End':

SHALL LIFE RENEW
THESE BODIES?
OF A TRUTH
ALL DEATH WILL HE ANNUL

This version of the lines totally reverses the intended effect of the words in the poem, which continues 'annul, all tears assuage?'. The questions are ironical, and the writer has no doubt that he is challenging the Christian code. Susan Owen must have known what she was doing, and, as Dominic Hibberd suggests (p. 194), she may have found it hard to dig out an appropriate quotation from Owen's mature poetry. This act of religiosity permanently undermines one's belief in her as a member of Owen's 'fit audience though few', for she had been the principal recipient of his poems and letters. Nevertheless she and her daughter faithfully kept, it seems, nearly all of Wilfred's letters, but in the strangest of places, not as an archive but more like the litter of a still-living presence. Even his revolver, which had been sent back with his personal effects, was found in a garden shed, still loaded, after her death (*CL* p. 1).

The other parent had also to perform certain duties for his son. On 16 April 1919, Owen having left no will, the administration of his estate was given to his father. Wilfred had left £162 13s, a sum which would have constituted roughly a year and a half's salary in an ordinary middle-class job, and probably consisted largely of back-pay. It may also have included his books and the few items of furniture which Owen had been assembling 'for a cottage' while he was in Scarborough.

The publication of the poems

A new reader might naturally think that the volume of collected or selected poems by Wilfred Owen which we are accustomed to using assembles texts which were immediately available at or shortly after the time of writing. This was not the case, and it is important at this stage, as we look back at the life so brutally cut off, to appreciate how few of Owen's poems had been published at the time of his death and how long it took to present a reasonable selection of his work to the public. He was diffident about showing his work around, and did not give everything he had written to Sassoon, for example. All might have been lost, and much was hidden away for years; on the other hand there were often several copies of the manuscripts in his careful handwriting. It was the quite remarkable impression he made on his contemporaries in the last year of his life, an impression of quiet confidence hiding amazing poetic power, that exacted their dedication to the task of getting his work into print; this in turn led to the determination of later editors to find more poems as time went by. But even then not all the poems that they found were printed. A complete edition of the poems and fragments was not available till 1983.

A further problem is editorial in a more technical sense: it is necessary to establish whether we are reading what Owen intended us to read. As has been explained, most of his poems were printed after his death from manuscripts; in many cases these include several drafts of a single poem. Sometimes each draft is full of corrections and afterthoughts. The final printed version of a poem is therefore an editorial construction, and some quite famous lines can begin to fade and dissolve before our eyes when we look at the critical edition by Jon Stallworthy, which prints all the manuscript readings.

Finally, because Owen was perceived as a war poet, it was difficult to know what to do with the many poems on other themes, with their frequent echoes of Swinburne and Wilde. These are generally considered to be either irrelevant or of poor quality. In the introduction to the Day-Lewis edition, for example, Owen's earlier work is judged to be 'vague, vaporous, subjective, highly "poetic" in a pseudo-Keatsian way, with Tennysonian and Ninety-ish echoes here and there: the verse of a youth in love with the idea of poetry – and in love with Love'.[1] In several editions such poems were not admitted or they were placed at the back of the volume. In fact, a good many of these minor poems are on erotic themes, and might provoke the reader to censor them or to regard them with distaste. It might have been easier if such poems were all 'early' – to be superseded by the bleaker vision of the war poet – but in fact Owen continued to produce these '1890s verses' while writing his more famous elegies of war. Many of these minor poems and fragments only appeared in public in Stallworthy's edition of 1983. Sassoon's first selection, it may be argued, was incisive because it was so brief.

The following poems were published in Owen's lifetime:

'Song of Songs', *The Hydra*, 1 September 1917
'The Next War', *The Hydra*, 29 September 1917
'Miners', *The Nation*, 26 January 1918
'Song of Songs', *The Bookman*, mid-May 1918 (it had been entered for a competition)
'Hospital barge at Cérisy' and 'Futility', *The Nation*, 15 June 1918

After his death the history of publication (before the major edition of 1963) is as follows:

1919: Seven poems in *Wheels*, an anthology edited by the Sitwells. This provided a Modernist rather than the Georgian context he might have expected for his work.
Various other single poems appeared in journals 1919–21
1920: *Poems* by Wilfred Owen, with an introduction by Sassoon, containing twenty-three poems
1921: *Poems* reprinted with one extra poem
1931: *The Poems of Wilfred Owen*, edited with a memoir and notes by Edmund Blunden.
1933: *Poems of Wilfred Owen* reprinted with corrections
1939: *Poems of Wilfred Owen* reprinted, and subsequently in 1946, 1949, 1951, 1955, 1960 and 1961
1963: *The Collected Poems of Wilfred Owen*, edited with an introduction and notes by C. Day-Lewis and with a memoir by Edmund Blunden.

What is to be noted in this brief outline of the publishing history of the poems is the gap between 1921 and 1931. I have in the past talked to survivors of the First World War and their relatives who have explained that Owen was not widely known in the 1920s and that their families were still being, in a sense, 'protected' – by War Office propaganda and visits from old comrades – from any unpatriotic sentiments or anything which would take away from the greatness of their victory and the heroism of their dead.

Mourning and the process of regeneration

Geoff Dyer's book on *The Missing of the Somme,* which was quoted from at the beginning of this section, is compelling reading, and particularly important because its author, born in 1958, is two generations from the war dead, and yet is profoundly affected by their loss. It is an elegiac study of the enduring strength which the Great War holds in our culture – he argues convincingly for a return to the description 'Great War' as opposed to 'WW1' or 'First World War'. Dyer also makes an interesting point about the way in which Owen's death was first received among his friends and contemporaries. He notes how Sassoon, in presenting the first collection of Wilfred Owen's *Poems* in 1920, decided to observe these guidelines:

> All that was strongest in Wilfred Owen survives in his poems; any superficial impressions of his personality, any records of his conversation, behaviour or appearance, would be irrelevant and unseemly. The curiosity which demands such morsels would be incapable of appreciating the richness of his work.[2]

This actually means that the poems should be presented without accompaniments which would obscure their stark message. The result, says Dyer, was that in the 1920s Owen was a disembodied voice, an oracle 'speaking from the other side of the grave'.[3] This is an unexpected point and represents a stage in the reception of Owen's poetry to which it is impossible for us to return.

In fact the creation of an image was not long delayed. The official journals duly reported Owen's death, sometimes with a photograph as was customary for officers. He had enlisted in the Artists' Rifles, and was included in their journal's Roll of Honour in January 1919:

4756 OWEN, Wilfred Edward Salter   Manchester

In 1919 Charles Scott Moncrieff, one of Owen's recent acquaintances, who seems to have presumed on their friendship in life as well as in death, produced a translation of *The Song of Roland.* This was originally to have been dedicated to Wilfred Owen. Scott Moncrieff tells us, in a draft preface of summer 1918,[4] that he had found

Owen's theory of assonance useful in matching up the effect of the similar line-endings which the chanson employs. Death made such a literary point superfluous. The book now opens with these words:

TO THREE MEN
SCHOLARS, POETS, SOLDIERS
WHO CAME TO THEIR RENCEVALS
IN SEPTEMBER, OCTOBER, AND NOVEMBER
NINETEEN HUNDRED AND EIGHTEEN
I DEDICATE MY PART IN A BOOK
OF WHICH THEIR FRIENDSHIP
QUICKENED THE BEGINNING
THEIR EXAMPLE HAS
JUSTIFIED THE CONTINUING

PHILIP BAINBRIGGE.
WILFRED OWEN.
IAN MACKENZIE.

This promotion of his friends to the status of heroes of old romance may seem exaggerated, but Scott Moncrieff's description of the period of summer 1918 'where the sound of the oliphant came so often and so direfully across the Channel' does ring true. The image may need expansion and clarification: at the most famous moment of the poem Roland sounds his horn.

CXXXV
The count Rollanz, though blood his mouth doth stain,
And burst are both the temples of his brain,
His oliphant he sounds with grief and pain:
Charles hath heard, listen the Franks again.
'That horn,' the King says, 'hath a mighty strain!'[5]

Owen is not to be compared with Roland in any literal way but the physicality of the description is curiously like the texture of the protest poems against the war. And it shows the process of poetic myth-making in operation. It will – later – seem a short step to the *In parenthesis* of David Jones, the epic poem of the Great War, with its undertext of mythological references.

Dyer is right in his thesis that Owen the man was absent in discussion of his work in the 1920s. It was Edmund Blunden who produced the first memoir of Wilfred Owen, which was prefixed to his 1931 edition of the poems. This was subsequently placed at the end of Day Lewis's edition. It is generally available and too long to be discussed here. It is also full of felicities of expression and sensible observations by one who had endured the same experiences in the Great War himself. Blunden concludes with great stress on Owen as a humanist and heir of the great Romantics:

He was, apart from Mr. Sassoon, the greatest of the English war poets. But the term 'war poets' is rather convenient than accurate. Wilfred Owen was a poet without classifications of war and peace. Had he lived, his humanity would have continued to encounter great and moving themes, the painful sometimes, sometimes the beautiful, and his art would have matched his vision. He was one of those destined beings who, without pride of self (the words of Shelley will never be excelled), 'see, as from a tower, the end of all'. Outwardly, he was quiet, unobtrusive, full of good sense; inwardly, he could not help regarding the world with the dignity of a seer.

Owen was preparing himself to the last moment in experience, observation, and composition for a volume of poems, to strike at the conscience of England . . .'[6]

I deliberately break off here. What actually happened was that Owen – who had fought – was adopted by the peace movement of the early 1930s as one of their father figures. Among other things the movement sought to ensure that the youth of England would never again be subject to carnage like that of the Great War. Although things changed with the rise of Hitler and the Civil War in Spain, it is often said that the generals of the Second World War were not prepared to put their troops through unnecessary set-piece battles. How far Owen and not the public memory of war influenced this may be debated, but Owen had already evolved into an admonitory figure whose work was well known. In any case the nature of warfare had changed completely, though set-piece battles did occur at Alamein and in Normandy. By the 1940s and 1950s Owen was becoming established as a school-text. His contemporaries, now grown older, began to write down their reminiscences.

Siegfried Sassoon, of course, had already done this in the 1930s with *Sherston's Progress*. This is essential reading, and describes his war service and his experiences at Craiglockhart (quoted from on p. 24). His new book of memoirs, *Siegfried's Journey*, which was published in 1946, describes his meeting with Owen and their poetic cooperation (see p. 25). What is now available for comparison is the actual text of his contemporary diary:

21 November 1917
Little Owen went to see Robbie [Ross] in town and made a very good impression. . . . I am sure he will be a very good poet some day and he is a very loveable creature.[7]

It is interesting to contrast this rather chirpy and patronising tone with the desolation of this extract from the memoir:

After the Armistice I waited to hear from him, not daring to ask myself, during those weeks of lively distraction, why no letter

arrived. Several months elapsed before I was told about his death.
I have never been able to accept that disappearance philosophic-
ally. A blank miserable sense of deprivation has dulled my mind
whenever I have thought of him, and even now it has needed an
effort of will to describe our friendship. Recognition of his poetry
has steadily increased, but the chasm in my private existence remains. I am unable to believe that 'whom the gods love die young.'[8]

A slightly glamorous sense of the period of youth irradiates Osbert
Sitwell's *Noble Essences*. People were different in the past from the
post-war (Second World War) present, yet Osbert tries to give hon-
esty to his first impressions of Wilfred Owen:

> there, in the comfortable warmth of Robbie's sitting-room, I saw
> a young officer of about my age – he was three months younger
> than myself – of sturdy, medium build, and wearing a khaki uni-
> form. His face was rather broad, and I think its most unusual
> characteristics were the width of eye and forehead, and the tawny,
> rather sanguine skin, which proclaimed, as against the message of
> his eyes – deep in colour and dark in their meaning – a love of life
> and a poet's enjoyment of air and light. His features were mobile
> but determined, and his hair short and of a soft brown. His whole
> appearance, in spite of what he had been through, gave the im-
> pression of being somewhat young for his age, and, though he
> seemed perfectly sure of himself, it was easy to perceive that by
> nature he was shy. He had the eager, supple good manners of the
> sensitive, and was eager and receptive, quick to see a point and
> smile. His voice – what does his voice sound like across the years?
> A soft modulation, even-toned, but with a warmth in it (I almost
> hear it now), a well-proportioned voice that signified a sense of
> justice and of compassion. With his contemporaries he talked at
> ease. Only in the presence of such literary nabobs of the period
> as Wells and Bennett could he scarcely bring himself to speak;
> and this silence, apart from being rooted in his natural modesty
> and good manners, was due, I think, to the immense esteem in
> which he held literature and those who practised the profession
> of author. His residence in France may have deepened this atti-
> tude of respect, and almost awe, which had in it nothing of the
> Englishman's casual approach to books. To him they were all-
> important, while poetry was the very crown of life, and constituted
> its meaning.[9]

Notice that there is still a faint hint of class distinction in both these
accounts, but this, it could be said in excusal, is of its time. A similar
process to the history of publication determined how Owen was
presented to the world after his death.

This has meant that by and large there has been an absence of negative criticism of Owen as a person until recently. For example, it is vital to the acceptance of the testimony provided by their poetry that both Sassoon and Owen, unlike the poet and musician Ivor Gurney, should be presented as normal (though all had been hospitalised as 'mental cases'); any suggestion that they were in reality sick would have immediately brought into question the reliability of their witness. Obviously Sassoon was never insane; he was a political detainee. Owen, on the other hand, had been diagnosed as suffering from neurasthenia.

A major problem which is involved in all this is the charge of cowardice. The source is some remarks by Robert Graves. Describing Sassoon's arrival at Craiglockhart, Graves mentions that:

> Another patient at the hospital was Wilfred Owen, who had had a bad time with the Manchester Regiment in France; and, further, it had preyed on his mind that he had been accused of cowardice by his commanding officer. He was in a very shaky condition.[10]

Here the problem is compounded by the unreliability of Graves in other places; his book caused several rows, and it is not easy to say how much he invented or, perhaps, wanted to annoy his audience. In fact, now that neurasthenia or battle-trauma has come to be regarded as normal after Vietnam and the Gulf, we would not see Owen's condition as a disgrace. A further point of contention is whether the charge of cowardice – if it is true – can be rebutted by proving that he went back to the front voluntarily in September 1918, and so redeemed himself in battle. The evidence would seem to suggest that he wanted to return to France, but in *The Last Year* Hibberd seems to question this. The poems are indecisive as witnesses.

Recently Pat Barker has emphasised the deep infliction of shell-shock on the soldiers of the Great War; in her fictional trilogy Sassoon and Owen appear as themselves, but are surrounded by some ghastly cases which serve to deepen the misery of the experience. All in all her compassion helps us to understand what Owen and the others must have gone through.[11]

Notes

1   *The Collected Poems of Wilfred Owen*, ed. C. Day-Lewis (London: Chatto and Windus, 1963), p. 11.
2   Wilfred Owen, *Poems*, ed. Siegfried Sassoon (London: Chatto and Windus, 1920), p. v.
3   Geoff Dyer, *The Missing of the Somme* (London: Penguin, 1995), p. 35.

4   The manuscript is reproduced in Hibberd, p. 117.
5   *The Song of Roland*, trans. C.K. Scott Moncrieff (London: Chapman and Hall, 1919), p. 59.
6   *Collected Poems*, ed. Day-Lewis, p. 179.
7   *Siegfried Sassoon: Diaries 1915–1918*, ed. Rupert Hart-Davis (London: Faber and Faber, 1983), p. 196.
8   Siegfried Sassoon, *Siegfried's Journey 1916–1920* (London: Faber and Faber, 1945), p. 72.
9   Osbert Sitwell, *Noble Essences or Courteous Revelations* (London: Macmillan, 1950), pp. 103–4.
10 Robert Graves, *Goodbye to All That* (London: Cape, 1931), p. 326.
11 See her trilogy: *Regeneration* (London: Viking, 1991), *The Eye in the Door* (London: Viking, 1993) and *The Ghost Road* (London: Viking, 1995).

Part Two
Cultural and Historical Background

4   The drift to war: 1890–1914

Individual experience is always comparatively easy to focus on, easy to absorb, easy, perhaps, to understand. But it is now necessary to put the individual life of Owen to one side and to see how his experience relates to that of other people – his contemporaries and in particular other poets. As we live our own lives we are only conscious in a limited way of our involvement with history; but those who come after us can see whether that life was typical or exceptional. Even if we cling to the idea that each life is unique, we can only justify that claim after making comparisons. And so, to put Owen's life into perspective, we need to go over the same ground again, looking at some aspects of the general experience.

Children in uniform

It might seem, with hindsight, that to anyone growing up in Britain in the years before 1914, the prospect of war was always present, and that a major conflict with Germany was inevitable as national rivalries reached points of crisis: this, after all, is how history is taught when one knows that the Great War was about to take place. But at the time it was not clear how far these agitations really affected the deeply peaceful state of mind which characterised the English people. There are no mentions of war-scares in Owen's letters; and one would not expect him to have taken up a teaching post in Bordeaux in 1913 if a European war was hourly expected.

But preparations for war had been in train for a long time; an arms race, which primarily affected the superiority of the British Navy, was supported by general acclaim. More subtly, all over Europe, the population was being accustomed to the wearing of uniform. This was not just in Prussia, considered to be the homeland of militarism, where uniforms were worn on public occasions and where the national character was assumed to be naturally pre-disposed to discipline and order – or arrogance and bellicosity, depending on your point of view. Even in Britain, after the initial débâcle of the Boer War, when national pride had been affronted, khaki-clad groups of civilians, gentler but no less militaristic, such as the Boy Scouts and the Territorial Army, rose to meet the challenge of the times, supported by the people's will.

These movements had a long ancestry. A corps of volunteers had always been available at moments of national danger; a good example is the invasion scare of 1859, when the threat came from France. Then the ideology underpinning the movement was liberal and nationalist: people were more enthused by Garibaldi and his Italian guerrillas than by a desire to be linked to the British Regular Army. The latter organisation, with its aristocratic officers and extremely low-class other ranks, was never popular, and, in any case, a large part of it was often out of the country on imperialistic engagements.

In the late Victorian period, then, propaganda was directed at the middle classes in ways that would redeem the associations of the Queen's uniform. Very young children wore sailor-suits and, less commonly, outfits that were versions of military dress. The Owen children were no exception. In one of the illustrations assembled by Jon Stallworthy for his biography, Wilfred appears in a rather jolly army uniform (JS p. 15); similar photographs from the family album show young Harold – prophetically – in a sailor-suit and Colin with a rifle (*CL* Plate III). This attempt to accustom children to uniform could simply be dismissed as a phase of fashion; its meaning would not have succeeded in permeating the deeper levels of the mind if the activity it represented had not been made sacred by the preaching of the Church.

The ideology of sacrifice

The difficulty in reconciling the apparent pacifism of Jesus, as presented in the New Testament, with the needs of the modern state has always been present. Later on, Edmund Blunden, who had a Christian education, used Article 37 of the Church of England as the epigraph to his Great War memoirs, *Undertones of War*: 'It is lawful for Christian men, at the commandment of the Magistrate, to wear weapons, and serve in the wars'. This terse directive, surely used ironically by Blunden, who knew what he was talking about, seems to gloss over a number of pertinent objections, and in the late nineteenth and early twentieth centuries, with a population largely unused to war, considerable efforts had to be made to re-align the teachings of Jesus to fit the demands of modern warfare. A huge number of volunteers would be required, and not all of these would return alive.

In spite of the progress of the Anglo-Catholic wing of the Church, the heart of English religion was still the Evangelical movement; Susan Owen and the Reverend Herbert Wigan had, after all, in their different ways, presented young Wilfred with this version of the Christian religion. Though it had originally come to maturity at the centre of national life during and after the Napoleonic Wars, it was not a movement which urged its adherents to spread the word by anything approaching military means. Preaching and missionary activity were the preferred methods, however much – to our more cynical eyes – it was an adjunct of Britain's drive to the conquest and colonisation of overseas territories.

Scenes of battle did, however, provide the background to some well-known hymns:

> The Son of God goes forth to war,
> A Kingly crown to gain;
> His blood-red banner streams afar: –
> Who follows in His train ?
>
> Bishop R. Heber

But the war was always received as a metaphorical one, and no serious enactment of the metaphor was proposed; this was probably a good thing in view of the later associations of the red flag. A rousing and memorable tune accompanied the verses of 'Onward Christian soldiers', which was less easy to interpret as entirely symbolic in its intentions; you were assumed to want to join in, and no guilt was attached to the adventure. On an occasion for marching this hymn could be sung out loud and clear; the drum could bang and the fife tootle away. Organisations such as the Boys' Brigade and the Church Lads' Brigade provided opportunities for this kind of healthy activity. But what had Jesus to do with the things which real soldiers would be required to do?

As time went on it was necessary to re-jig some well-known sayings, for example:

> Greater love hath no man than this, that a man lay down his life for his friends. (St John xv, 13)

This perfectly straightforward moral observation was now twisted so that it encompassed both going to war (on behalf of the civilian population) and acts of heroism on the battlefield. It was not made clear how bayonets, grenades and other offensive personal weapons were to be used by the Christian combatant in the act of 'laying down one's life'; what was portrayed was an act of sacrifice. Nor was it explained how the use of large-scale means of destruction such as artillery fitted in to this concept; these were simply background noise, like the sound-effects of a play. The casualness of death produced by such explosive devices was a problem and seemed to have no meaning; the God who cared for the fall of a sparrow could hardly intervene on these occasions. One begins to realise why, later on, the troops fell back upon fatalistic beliefs: 'That shell will only hurt you if it's got your name written on it'.

If directly challenged on these points, the Church's spokesman could refine the opposition's words to extend the ideal of self-sacrifice that the Bible appeared to be advocating:

War is not murder, as some fancy; war is sacrifice. The fighting and killing are not of the essence of it, but are the accidents, though the inseparable accidents; and even these, in the wide modern fields where a soldier rarely in his own sight sheds any blood but his own, where he lies on the battle sward not to inflict death but to endure it – even these are mainly purged of savagery and transfigured into devotion. War is not murder but sacrifice, which is the soul of Christianity.[1]

This was a normal, not untypical position to take, especially among those instructing the young.

Owen's mature view on all this is worth mentioning here. When asked to give lectures on such themes in December 1917, he refused, telling his mother that 'it is a Jesuitical movement to catch 'em young, and prepare them for the Eucharist of their own blood' (*CL* p. 516). He also exposed the kind of preaching quoted above in the 'Parable of the Old Man and the Young', showing that these excessively warlike individuals neither wished for nor required God's mercy. These issues will be more fully explored in Chapter 9.

Note

1 National Service League 'Leaflet L', *Religious Thought and National Service* (1903), quoted in Anne Summers, 'Militarism in Britain before the Great War', *History Workshop Journal* 2, Autumn 1976, pp. 104–23, in which many of the ideas in this section are fully discussed.

5 The course of the war in outline from a British point of view

Such was the success of this propaganda that any appeals to political liberalism or the international solidarity of the working classes, though they were made, seemed merely superficial when the call actually came. People queued to be enrolled in the armed forces in August and September 1914. An example may be found in the autobiographical account by George Coppard:

> Towards the end of August I presented myself to the recruiting sergeant at Mitcham Road Barracks, Croydon. There was a steady stream of men, mostly working types, queueing up to enlist. The sergeant asked me my age, and when told, replied, 'Clear off son. Come back tomorrow and see if you're nineteen, eh?' So I turned up again the next day and gave my age as nineteen. I attested in a batch of a dozen others and, holding up my right hand, swore to fight for King and Country. The sergeant winked as he gave me the King's shilling, plus one shilling and ninepence ration money for that day. I believe he also got a shilling for each man he secured as a recruit.
>
> I see from my discharge paper that I enlisted on 27th August 1914. As I was born on 26th January 1898, it follows that I was sixteen years and seven months old.[1]

Few people saw beyond this. It seemed a splendid opportunity to slip the leash, to escape the monotony of urban life and to find a chance for adventure. One feature of the enlistment was that friends or relatives could serve together; whole towns were represented by their 'lads', who marched away together in the 'Pals Brigades'.

Britain's entry into the Great War was triggered by the German invasion of Belgium. A treaty of 1839 guaranteed Belgian neutrality, and Britain was one of the guarantors; this commitment was presented to the British public as a matter of honour. More general problems of strategy were neither explored nor explained; it was clear that the Navy would control the Channel, but once across how was Britain's tiny regular Army supposed to cope with the problem? Luckily the system of alliances meant that Britain would line up with two great land powers, France and Russia; these would hold back the combined forces of Austria-Hungary and Germany. But the Germans would have to fight on two fronts, so their strategy was to repeat the success of 1870 and deal with France as rapidly as possible.

45

The German attack on Belgium was a necessary part of the plan, known as the 'Schlieffen plan', which was meant to secure the fall of Paris within six weeks. (Count von Schlieffen was a German general who had proposed this venture as early as 1895; by 1914 he was dead.) The route of the armies through Belgium would outflank the defences along the Franco-German border; it was assumed that the Belgians would capitulate. However, when the attack came they resisted the advance bravely, first at Liège and later at Antwerp, and so succeeded in gaining time. This enabled the French to move up into southern Belgium, and the British Expeditionary Force to push forward as far as Mons, before running unexpectedly into the German advance. In this first battle of the war the British Army distinguished itself by unleashing rapid rifle-fire which the Germans assumed came from machine-guns. The legend that the angels fought on the British side is further evidence of the religiosity which permeated war-propaganda.

In fact this was only a holding action in a war of movement; the German advance continued until Paris was threatened. By this time the instructions of von Schlieffen had begun to get muddled, and the Germans began to lose the initiative. After a brilliant stroke by the French general Galliéni, who used the taxis of Paris to move an army, the German forces were halted at the Battle of the Marne. The Allies were able to push them back, and eventually the front was stabilised as a long line of trenches, running from the Belgian coast to the Swiss border. By the end of 1914 the British forces were concentrated in Flanders, holding on to a salient, or bulge in the line, to the east of Ypres (pronounced 'Wipers' by the troops), the last Belgian town of any importance to remain in Allied hands. In actuality the salient was a flat area of land surrounded by slight eminences which the Germans had occupied, giving them a splendid view of the British defences. It would have been more sensible to vacate the salient and move back to the canal and river systems which the Belgians had been able to exploit in the far west of the front; but as always it was more important to maintain the fiction that the Allies controlled a large area of strategic ground. This would lead to immense problems in the future.

Of course there were always plans to move out of these 'temporary' trenches and to continue a war of movement, but they rarely came to fruition. In April 1915 the Germans used gas for the first time, north of Ypres, and under its cover mounted a major attack on the salient, reducing it by half. Their real forward movement was about two miles. Later in the year the British attacked at Loos, near Lille; in some places they made gains of about three miles, which threw the Germans into a momentary panic. These figures show the reduced scale of the gains now achievable in this kind of warfare. In

Presented with "Fashions for All," Christmas 1915.

THE ANGELS OF MONS.

Print from the painting titled *The Angels of Mons* by W.H. Margetson
Reproduced with the permission of The Imperial War Museum,
London

fact the troops were pinned down all along the Western Front by heavy artillery duels; the shells flew over their heads continually. The machine-gun prevented any movement at close range. From all this the Germans learnt the need for deep dugouts and concrete bastions; the Allies were slow to invest in anything more than wood and sandbags for a long time, and were soon working in the mire caused by rain and winter weather. Shells destroyed whatever drainage system had previously existed.

A diversion of activity for the Australians, British and French in 1915 was the proposal to attack Turkey through the Dardanelles. Nominally this was about sending reinforcements to Russia, but a deeper plan – to seize portions of the Turkish Empire – was already maturing. A surprise naval breakthrough intended to penetrate as far as Constantinople might have succeeded, but was called off too soon. Landings were therefore made in the general area of Gallipoli; the beaches were unsuitable because the Turks could keep the Allies under permanent surveillance from the hills above them. As on the Western Front, the troops learned to endure the hazards of this exposed trench-system without questioning the wisdom of their generals. The whole enterprise was abandoned early in 1916.

Meanwhile the French, who garrisoned most of the line of trenches in the west, were trying to hold on to their salient at Verdun. There were massive German assaults in early 1916; the losses were appalling on both sides. It had now become a matter of honour, of French prestige as much as strategy. The British were encouraged to provide a diversion, and Haig, who was now in charge, decided that Ypres was not the best place for this. Many British soldiers were therefore assembled at a new point in the line – the River Somme. The battle-plan commenced with the most massive artillery bombardment in history; fire was concentrated on the German barbed wire and trenches for five days. The British troops were told that the wire would be destroyed and that anything living would have ceased to exist. On 1 July 1916 they were ordered to advance in long lines at a walking pace; they were carrying full kit. There would be no opposition. In an act of bravado one officer dribbled a football. The Germans, who had survived in their deep concrete dugouts, came up when the bombardment ceased, and could not believe their eyes. Not only had their wire survived – it simply rose in the air and fell back – but their enemy could be seen in full view in broad daylight. (Usually attacks took place at dawn or dusk.) They set up their machine-guns and with traversing fire mowed down the British troops in swathes. There were 60,000 casualties on the first day. Whole companies had disappeared; in the worst cases whole regiments had ceased to exist as proper fighting forces.

The battle then continued day after day, though the ground gained was in most areas quite negligible. The evidence of the incompetence of the British generals really began with this battle. The plan was inane, but far worse was the decision to continue when its failure was so obvious. The more intelligent junior officers and men began to regard their commanders as not just incompetent but criminal, and no amount of revisionist special pleading in recent histories can ever excuse them. When the battle came to a halt after six months, half a million men had been lost on the British side and roughly the same number of Germans. It was in this year that the British finally introduced conscription, though it is still a matter of debate whether this was really necessary (Owen, one recalls, had volunteered at the end of 1915). Militarisation seemed to have involved the whole country and women were expected to 'do their bit'. They took over many of the peacetime roles usually occupied by men, e.g. bus driving, and were recruited into the Women's Auxiliary Army Corps (WAAC). Owen found in 1917 that the WAAC were serving meals at Craiglockhart, and in 1918 they had taken over Mess Duties at Scarborough. The Pals Brigades no longer featured in the general recruiting strategy; in any case many of them had disappeared in the blood-letting of the Somme.

As has been pointed out, Owen came to join the Manchesters early in 1917 at the tail end of this battle, and witnessed the Germans' planned withdrawal in this sector. They fell back to the recently constructed and seemingly impregnable Hindenburg line, so saving themselves unnecessary stress in holding on to the extended salient in this area. This was no victory for the British at all. The Germans could always retake the ground they had apparently lost, and did when the occasion came. Meanwhile in the north, while Owen was back home in hospital, the British, Canadians and Australians embarked upon the Third Battle of Ypres. The aim was to re-establish the salient from which they had been largely driven in 1915. They finally reached Passchendaele, approximately 10 kilometres from Ypres, in December 1917, after a prolonged process of attrition in which roughly a quarter of a million men were lost on each side.

The year closed with some indications of hope. The Americans had entered the war on 2 April, and their troops were beginning to arrive. Secondly, the tank, a British invention which was intended to cross trenches without difficulty, was beginning to show its usefulness, being highly successful in the Battle of Cambrai. On the other side of Europe, however, the news was bad: the Russian war-machine had collapsed and, after the October Revolution, Lenin sued for peace.

This at last freed the Germans from the necessity of having to fight on two fronts; reinforcements were transferred from Russia to France. In March 1918 there was a surprise breakthrough near St

Quentin and the Germans reoccupied the area they had evacuated in early 1917. As Owen said in a letter: 'It is specially cruel for me to hear of all *we* gained by St. Quentin having been lost. They are dying again at Beaumont Hamel, which already in 1916 was cobbled with skulls' (*CL* p. 542). The rapid advance continued; the German army now moved into previously unoccupied territory and appeared to be making for the Channel. When the news broke it caused a panic at home, and all fit and available military personnel were sent out. Owen reports that he had heard from Scarborough that 'of the 100 officers now in Clarence Gardens, *53* are going out immediately, and practically the whole of the men . . .' (*CL* p. 545).

A second German offensive opened near Ypres, then a third in the south, leading to the Second Battle of the Marne. But by July 1918 the tide had turned. First the French and Americans began to recapture territory, aided by tanks; then, on 8 August, the British attacked near Amiens – the occasion was later called 'the black day of the German Army'. By the time Owen rejoined his regiment in September the British advance was rolling back the German lines. When the armistice came into effect on 11 November British troops had just arrived at Mons, where their war had begun in 1914.

Total war and the manipulation of the 'truth'

A number of more general points need to be made to supplement this necessarily brief account. They are mainly concerned with communications – between the press and the civilian population, between different groups of soldiers, and finally between soldiers and civilians.

As the war continued the initial optimism of a 'war that would be over by Christmas' rapidly faded. Truth was, as always, the first casualty, and soon became a very relative commodity. Of course there was the need to control the flow of information in order to baffle the enemy, but this rapidly turned into disinformation and outright invention. War propaganda on the Allied side was particularly mischievous from the earliest days; the Germans were accused of atrocities in Belgium – 'the bayonetting of babies', for example – which had no basis in fact but were very persistently held to. The occasional real atrocity, for example the execution by shooting of Edith Cavell, a British nurse who had stayed in Brussels and was accused of assisting fugitives in their escape, was never forgotten.

Little criticism of the conduct of the war by the Allies was allowed to surface, though Churchill was disgraced after the failure of the Dardanelles expedition. The soldiers in the first years of the war had been volunteers, and so were automatically heroes of a kind; the quality most in demand was endurance, but not all could endure.

The fact that there were executions for cowardice in the trenches, for example, was not widely known until the revelations of Victor Sylvester, which were shown on television in the 1980s; more understanding of the effects of battle-trauma has led to attempts to secure rehabilitations in recent years, and redeem the honour of these dead soldiers for their families.

After 1916 the atmosphere of the war changed for the worse; the introduction of conscription alienated those who still believed in liberal values, and strengthened the moral basis of the embryonic peace movement. Tensions developed between the various groups of participants in the war effort. First of all, as has already been indicated, the soldiers and officers who fought in the trenches despised the senior officers who stayed well behind the lines and were responsible for the 'strategy' of the Somme and similar battles.

Secondly, the soldiers found little awareness of the conditions in the trenches when they went on leave, and misunderstood those who may have felt that the attempt to maintain the appearance of normality at home would be what the soldiers wanted. We have noted that Owen did not feel that his father understood what appalling experiences he had gone through, and though we do not have Susan Owen's letters it may be deduced from her son's replies that he was subjected to a barrage of hypochondriacal fantasy with seemingly little appreciation of his own real illness. His last letter ends 'I think of you always in bed', which, although not intended as a criticism, tells us a lot. The soldiers' particular hatred was directed at those 'who had done well out of the war', manufacturers and of course politicians and their lackeys, in particular Horatio Bottomley. It was Sassoon who focused the anger felt against the ignorant civilians: a poem, 'Blighters', about a London music-hall audience delighting in crude jingoism, climaxes in

> I'd love to see a Tank come down the stalls,
> Lurching to rag-time tunes, or 'Home, sweet Home',
> And there'd be no more jokes in Music-halls
> To mock the riddled corpses round Bapaume.

The soldiers took refuge in less savage humour and irony, usually too obscene to be reported accurately at the time. Even in the worst parts of the front line there was a wish to joke and to make the best of a bad job (see *The Wipers Times*). While this must be admired, such self-censorship could also be described as a typically British way of avoiding the unpleasantness of the truth.

A final point is to notice that although war propaganda persisted in inflaming national hatreds, the ordinary soldiers on either side felt they had more in common with their opposite numbers than they had with some of their officers or with the civilians at home. Such

A Scots guardsman giving a drink from his water-bottle to a wounded German prisoner, August 1918

feelings led to images such as that illustrated here of a Scots guardsman giving a drink to a German prisoner, taken in the later stages of the war.

While all photographs at the time were in some sense posed, one has to ask whether such an action would have been performed to order. All in all, it provides a standing rebuke to the Bottomleys of the world, and offers a hope of final reconciliation, which Owen himself described in his own way in 'Strange Meeting'.

Note

1   George Coppard, *With a Machine Gun to Cambrai* (London: Imperial War Museum, 1969), p. 1.

6 Images: the artist and truth

It is possible to see the tensions discussed in the previous chapter quite clearly in pictures of the period, especially in the work of the 'war artists', who were commissioned to record the war in paintings. Often trained in the romantic landscape tradition, they found it difficult to accommodate to the scenery of battle without changing their style. On the other hand they found they could not honestly produce the propaganda which was at first expected from them and tried to show what they had seen. The work of the more famous war artists can only be mentioned here as there is no reason to suppose that Owen would have seen the work of John and Paul Nash, for example; their vision came to fruition in paintings that were made while Owen was writing his poems, and many were exhibited after the war was over. In looking at paintings from earlier in the war we shall encounter difficulties because the later examples are so famous. It is not easy to understand the oblique way in which some of the earlier artists deal with the war; for a civilian painter it was not easy to speak out, as the general public were not yet conditioned to receive any radical departure from sentimental narrative paintings.

Some of the images that did gain general approval can be illustrated from popular art of the time, especially postcards, posters and sheet music-covers. An example is the illustration on p. 47 of *The Angels of Mons*, which capitalises on a famous story of the battlefield. Harold Begbie[1] found British nurses who had seen strange figures looking after wounded soldiers; the soldiers themselves had seen lights in the sky and said they had been aided by supernatural beings. For the postcard artist there were no difficulties in such manipulation of religious imagery; rather, people wished to believe that the story was true. Here one could see clear evidence that God was on the side of the British; of course to the Germans he was on their side too. Of all the heavenly host, angels were perhaps the most military personages. There is no way of proving that Wilfred Owen saw or did not see such popular images, but they were generally available. It is worth pointing out, though, that angels in Owen's poetry can be hostile. In 'Soldier's Dream' Jesus stops the fighting by destroying the weaponry of war with his tears:

> But God was vexed, and gave all power to Michael;
> And when I woke he'd seen to our repairs.

Images from fine art were not distributed so widely; in peacetime Owen, who was interested in painting, would have seen engravings or possibly photographic reproductions of important new pictures, but his absence in France might have made this difficult. When he was able to get to London he regularly visited the Royal Academy summer exhibitions and was there in 1916 and 1917 when the paintings discussed below were on display. In looking at these pictures (which Owen did not comment on) it is not the intention to establish sources for Owen's poetic imagery; only to show themes in general circulation which might parallel those in his poetry.

Here I propose to look first at the case of Charles Sims, whose career is outlined in the biographical section of this book. Sims was famous for his symbolist pictures and for his evocative English landscapes. *Clio and the Children* was begun in 1913; it was intended to be his Diploma work for the Royal Academy. The downland in the background shows that the scene is set in Sussex, then regarded as the most English of counties, being praised by Kipling and Belloc. Originally a more upright version of Clio, who is the Muse of History, was to be seen on the right reading the lessons of history from a scroll; the children were presumably taking it all in for their own good. But Sims's eldest son was killed in the war during 1915; in his distress he altered the painting. Now the Muse of History pauses while reading the annals. Clio is unable to face the children's attentive gaze. She bows her head in grief and the scroll falls from her hand, revealing a large stain of blood, which blots out the year she has reached. As Richard Cork points out, this 'proved too extreme for the critics who had admired his once lyrical art';[2] they rejected the stricken figure of Clio, who was seen as 'merely irrelevant' by *The Times* and a 'blemish' by *The Connoisseur*. These judgements tell us more about the reviewers than about the painting. People were unable to accept the idea that the historical record had in any way been mutilated by the war.

For at that time a picture which had not merely been exhibited at the Royal Academy, but accepted by it as a Diploma work, could not be seen as an image of personal tragedy; it had become a public, not a private document. The beauty of landscape for which Sims had been praised is still there, but now the whole setting seems ironic. The picture quietly destroys illusions of human grandeur; this is the disappointment we have come to after a century of Progress. It announces to the world the impact of the appalling news from France.

The painting also highlights the problem of communication – how exactly are we going to tell the children and what are we going to tell them? Here the messages in this picture seem to gloss exactly the points that Owen made in 'Dulce et Decorum Est':

Clio and the Children, 1913–15, Charles Sims
Royal Academy of Arts, London

My friend, you would not tell with such high zest
To children ardent for some desperate glory,
The old Lie: Dulce et decorum est
Pro patria mori.

and in 'Strange Meeting':

None will break ranks, though nations trek from progress

– a statement which would have seemed far more shocking at the time than it does now. The idyllic background of southern England also recalls a strange remark in a letter already quoted: Owen, still recovering from his own battle-trauma, tells Gunston after a visit to Winchester, 'I could almost see the dead lying about in the hollows of the downs' (*CL* p. 508). Here both the background to the painting and the unexpectedness of Owen's remark attempt to bring home to the English heartland the truth about what was happening in the war.

A painting with allusions to Classical mythology may have been too subtle for the wider public. There were no such difficulties with Christianity; the 1916 exhibition also included *Youth Mourning* by George Clausen. There were two versions of this painting. In the earlier version, as seen by Owen, there are three white crosses prominent in the foreground. An empty level plain stretches into the distance, emphasising the isolation of the mourner. In the distance groups of identical white crosses like military cemeteries of the time can be seen at intervals, though only two are clearly visible. Once again there is a personal reference as it is likely 'that it was inspired by the death in the war of his daughter's fiancé'. The fact that the mourner is naked, with her face turned away from the viewer, takes away the personal element and gives her a universal significance.

In the other version, painted twelve years later, which is all we now have, there is a single cross of darker wood. The distant landscape has been transformed with black-looking pools which suggest a water-logged battle-zone in northern France or Belgium. The whole painting seems a fitting companion-piece to Owen's 'Anthem for Doomed Youth':

The pallor of girls' brows shall be their pall;
Their flowers the tenderness of patient minds . . .

The next picture was shown by Sims at the Royal Academy in 1917. The figure of the wounded soldier is cleverly supported on fence-rails which pun on the cross of Christ's Passion. In the same way the people surrounding him are a visual pun on the Holy Family. Once again, there was something more shocking then about this picture than we can imagine now. Though the painting was noticed by many at the exhibition, Owen does not comment on it, but then

Youth Mourning, 1916 (original version), George Clausen
Taken from *Royal Academy Illustrated*, 1916: Royal Academy of Arts,
London

he took a very cursory glance at the whole show. We can see many
parallels in Owen's poems and letters, for example:

> For 14 hours yesterday I was at work – teaching Christ to lift his
> cross by numbers, and how to adjust his crown; and not to ima-
> gine he thirst until after the last halt; I attended his Supper to see
> that there were no complaints; and inspected his feet to see that

Greater love hath no man, 1917, Charles Sims
By permission of the Bodleian Library, University of Oxford (shelf-mark: Per 1707 d 73)

they should be worthy of the nails. I see to it that he is dumb and
stands to attention before his accusers. With a piece of silver I buy
him every day, and with maps I make him familiar with the to-
pography of Golgotha. (*CL* p. 562)

'Greater love' has by this stage of the war become a kind of cliché
and the picture may have been intended to reinvigorate the message. Actually its curiously dream-like suspension of action, and the
circular frame, which resembles a peep-hole, may suggest that the
soldier – who is doing the guarding or the laying down of life on this
side of the fence – is not visible to the family, who appear to be
looking at something beyond the viewer.

Of more clinical interest is the series of studies made by Henry
Tonks of wounded soldiers. Tonks had been a surgeon before the
war and joined the Royal Army Medical Corps at the age of sixty.
These drawings were never publicly shown till years after the war,
and are really intended to be accurate studies for purely medical
purposes. As Richard Cork says: 'He believed that the curiosity

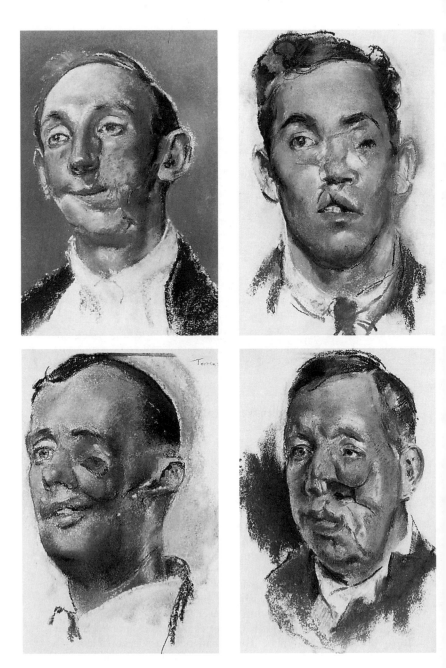

Studies of Facial Wounds, 1916, Henry Tonks
Reproduced by kind permission of the President and Council of the
Royal College of Surgeons of England

60

aroused by his work was morbid, even though the pastels now seem admirable in their frank yet tender depiction of the soldiers' battered faces'.[3] The sketches may be compared to the photographs of wounded men which Owen used to carry about in order to shock civilians;[4] the poems such as 'Disabled', 'Mental Cases' and 'À Terre' may be considered to have the same effect.

Summing up, the quality Wilfred Owen looked for in such images was the truth, and he reacted strongly to staged or manipulated versions of it. Cork explains one of Owen's few excursions into art criticism. The very first war artist, Muirhead Bone, produced lightning sketches of the Somme offensive which were intended for propaganda purposes. Wilfred wrote to his mother after first-hand experience of the front: 'Those "Somme Pictures" are the laughing stock of the army – like the trenches on exhibition at Kensington' (*CL* p. 429).

Notes

1 Harold Begbie, *On the Side of the Angels. The Story of the Angel at Mons. An Answer to 'The Bowmen'* (London: Hodder and Stoughton, 1915). The bowmen referred to are 'The Bowmen of Agincourt', a story by Arthur Machen which is usually taken to be the source of the legend.

2 Richard Cork, *A Bitter Truth: Avant-Garde Art and the Great War* (New Haven and London: Yale University Press, 1994), p. 129.

3 Cork, *A Bitter Truth*, p. 138.

4 Some doubt has been cast upon the existence of these photographs by Dominic Hibberd, who analyses the evidence and calls the whole story a 'legend' See *Owen the Poet* (London: Macmillan, 1986), p. 129. But such photographs were vividly remembered by Harold Owen. My source is a letter from John Bell (March 1998).

7 The poetry of the Great War down to 1917

Any attempt to survey the poetry of the Great War must come to terms with its volume and diversity; as has often been remarked, it was a very literary war. In this very selective overview, discussion will normally be limited to texts which Owen may be assumed to have read or at least heard about. By so doing it may be possible to establish the background against which he emerged as a war poet.

In some ways it is easier to discover what Owen had read than one might expect, as he left behind a library which has been preserved intact. There are also reading lists which he occasionally set himself to work through. He would also have seen many poems in magazines and newspapers, and sometimes recorded his reactions to them. Nevertheless a note of caution is necessary. Many famous poems which we would associate with the Great War were not published – or even written – until the war was over, and the inclusion of these in anthologies can give a false impression of what poetry was available to readers at the time.

The standard collections – then and now – keep to a middle- or officer-class view of what poetry is; it is important to realise that not only public-school boys wrote verse, though admittedly theirs is where the intellectual strength of the earlier war poetry is to be found. Brian Gardner, in compiling one of the best of the anthologies, *Up the Line to Death* (1964), tried to extend the definition of war poetry to include extracts from the songs with which the troops regaled themselves. While some of the more popular efforts seem to have dated, others have acquired a terrible resonance beyond the time they commemorate:

> We're here because we're here
> Because we're here, because we're here . . .

now seems to carry echoes of the last stand of King Harold's army at the Battle of Hastings as well as looking forward to the miners' defiant chanting as they were beaten down at the Battle of Orgreave in 1984. The genre was further extended to include women's verse in *Scars upon my heart*, selected by Catherine Reilly (1981); she found an enormous number of unknown writers in her work as a librarian. When grouped together in a library the collections of tiny memorial volumes, often published at parental expense, add to the sadness of it all as well as explaining why so much was preserved. The sheer immensity of all this verse can give the impression that everybody

was involved. Those not actually engaged in writing were either singing songs, reading verses in the dug-out, or acting as critical audience to first drafts of what were to become famous poems. Recitation
was also in demand. Poor Blunden had on occasion to perform
before the generals.

Short poems will comprise the subject matter of this survey. Long
poems – together with memoirs, novels and plays – came later, and
are more reflective, more concerned with 'meanwhile' and 'on the
other hand'. The advantage of the short poem, which at that time
must be seen as a direct descendant of the Romantic lyric, is that it
can immortalise a moment of action or concern, or capture a point
of view which is temporary and evanescent. In the work of these
poets, rather than in the more famous 'inscapes' of Gerard Manley
Hopkins or the 'epiphanies' of James Joyce,[1] can be found, with
terrible ironies, the true inheritance of Walter Pater. As outlined in
the programme for living which concluded his book on *The Renaissance*, they burn, briefly, 'with [a] hard gem-like flame'; anticipating
the shortness of the life before them they seem to live out his doc-
trine without realising it:

> While all melts under our feet, we may well catch at any exquisite
> passion, or any contribution to knowledge that seems by a lifted
> horizon to set the spirit free for a moment. . . . With this sense of
> the splendour of our experience and of its awful brevity, gathering
> all we are into one desperate effort to see and touch, we shall hardly
> have time to make theories about the things we see and touch.[2]

The very temporariness of existence for these poets can still shock:
they begin to sing and are cut off in mid-sentence, as it were. Too
much discussion of their individual lives, in the Romantic biographical tradition, has little to offer: one lists their schools, their higher
education or lack of it, their experience of battle. Most were Second
Lieutenants, whose duty was to lead the troops into battle or more
often on a dismal raid into no man's land; the expectation of life for
a junior officer in the front-line trenches was two weeks. Of course,
many did survive the war, but sometimes lapsed into silence, like
F.W. Harvey, who became a country solicitor; others never recovered
their mental stability, and were incarcerated in asylums, like Ivor
Gurney; or, so permanently marked by what they had been through,
like Edmund Blunden, they became haunted men. So, though many
names, some famous, some otherwise, crowd into the pages of any
anthology and ask to be evaluated as individuals, what is important
is their joint testimony. It is as if the experience of the war was
recorded by all the poets in a kind of collective diary.

The poets come and go, as it were, but our real subject is what
happens to the poetic discourse of the English language. Owen hinted

63

at more than he realised when he wrote to his mother, well before enlisting: 'Do you know what would hold me together on a battle-field? The sense that I was perpetuating the language in which Keats and the rest of them wrote!' (*CL* p. 300).

Many quite minor poets celebrated the mood of 1914, and, without putting themselves forward, encouraged other civilians to join up. Even the young George Orwell, then still known as Eric Blair, felt moved to contribute some stanzas to the press, which conclude:

> Awake ! Oh you young men of England,
> For if when your country's in need,
> You do not enlist by the thousand,
> You truly are cowards indeed.[3]

He was then aged eleven. More interesting is 'The Volunteer' by Herbert Asquith, the son of the Prime Minister. It had apparently been written two years before the war, and was therefore available for publication on 8 August 1914. The poem describes the romantic military dreams of a city clerk, no longer young, who is now able to fulfil these wishes. It concludes:

> His lance is broken; but he lies content
> With that high hour in which he lived and died.
> And falling thus, he wants no recompense
> Who found his battle in the last resort;
> Nor needs he any hearse to bear him hence,
> Who goes to join the men of Agincourt.[4]

The mock-Shakespearian and chivalric echoes are splendidly if sadly invoked, echoing the mood of the time; later on in the war Owen will find both ironies and regrets in the contrast between the Middle Ages and the present (see 'Hospital Barge', p. 92).

By 1915 the war poem had indeed become a recognised genre with an unashamedly patriotic message and a national audience. Owen saw *The Times* supplement of *War Poems from The Times, August 1914–15* while still in Bordeaux (*CL* p. 355). Besides the established poets, Robert Bridges, Rudyard Kipling and Thomas Hardy, this contained Laurence Binyon's 'For the Fallen' and 'Into Battle' by Julian Grenfell, both of which have now entered into the national psyche; by this I mean that they are not simply part of our literary heritage but have become popular pieces of recitation for the appro-priate occasions, like sections of the Bible or 'Abide with me'. At the time Owen noticed the Binyon poem but gave more praises to Newbolt and Dudley Clark. Though these sentiments were dashed off on a postcard to Leslie Gunston, it shows how much Owen's taste was still in line with the mood of the nation.

Of the younger generation the first poet of any talent to engage with the war was Rupert Brooke. His '1914 sonnets', after being read from the pulpit of St Paul's Cathedral by Dean Inge on Easter Sunday 1915, became universally known, and Owen possessed a copy of *1914 and Other Poems* in the edition of May 1916. Brooke is worth discussing at some length both for the fact that his was a major contribution to the canon of war poems, and because his education and early work seem to point in a quite opposite direction to the famous sonnets. His Cambridge background (he was a fellow of King's College) may have influenced him in his sympathy with 'left-wing' movements before the war. He was a Fabian Socialist, a friend of Virginia Woolf and an associate of the Bloomsbury Group. His earlier poetry is experimental and is several years ahead of most of the other poets, including Owen of course, in its retreat from high-flown Victorian moralising and its use of colloquial diction. In describing Brooke as one of the best of the Georgians, it is important to realise that the reputation of this school of poets suffered so much from the advent of Modernism that even today it is difficult to avoid seeing the name as a term of abuse. Historically the Georgians were almost an adjunct of the Liberal party which had come to power in 1906; in another sense of the word they were liberal intellectuals. They were forward-looking poets who thought they had freed themselves from Victorianism; they had ditched its cultural baggage and felt they were in harmony with the new reign. In 1912 the first anthology of *Georgian Poetry* appeared, edited by Edward Marsh, a powerful civil servant, who was Private Secretary to Churchill. The fact that Brooke merits four poems in this volume is evidence of his perceived status.

The '1914 sonnets' grew as much out of frustration as out of patriotism. This sub-text is exposed in their personal associations and in what close analysis of the language seems to reveal. Brooke's poems, in which at times he wrestles with his own preoccupations, were deliberately used by Winston Churchill and others as patriotic propaganda; in this context they are wrenched almost 180 degrees from their true direction. The fact that they capture a particular moment of our history was recognised by many others, who felt that they shared Brooke's emotions. Their documentary value is not in doubt. Perhaps it would be better to look at one in detail to understand what is going on.

1914 – III. THE DEAD

Blow out, you bugles, over the rich Dead!
  There's none of these so lonely and poor of old,
  But, dying, has made us rarer gifts than gold.
These laid the world away; poured out the red

Sweet wine of youth; gave up the years to be
   Of work and joy, and that unhoped serene,
   That men call age; and those who would have been,
Their sons, they gave, their immortality.
Blow, bugles, blow! They brought us, for our dearth,
   Holiness, lacked so long, and Love, and Pain.
Honour has come back, as a king, to earth,
   And paid his subjects with a royal wage;
And Nobleness walks in our ways again;
   And we have come into our heritage.

It is impossible to deny the power of this poem and what it tries to do. Its ancestors are Wordsworth's and Milton's patriotic sonnets, though curiously those poets could at their greatest moments write more colloquially than Brooke succeeds in doing here. He is consciously embarking on an exercise in high-flown sentiment to which he is not used and from the second to the eighth line he seems to stumble and hesitate slightly; one could argue that he is trying to convince himself as much as others what is to be done. Then in the sestet the poem is set to run towards full closure with settled stride. We seem to hear the voice of conviction and are ourselves persuaded that everything he says is true. It is like being exhorted at a Revivalist meeting. We take the leap of faith, and are healed; as Brooke said in the sonnet 'Peace', we are 'as swimmers into cleanness leaping'.

It is only when we look closely at what is really being said that we begin to wake up. In English schools this poem used to be regularly destroyed by teachers, desperate to get their pupils to see what was camouflaged under the term 'red sweet wine of youth', and what to expect as a 'royal wage'; but, as Welland has pointed out (p. 16), Brooke is not alone in his use of inflated rhetoric. The poetry of 1914 is generally of this kind and must be read as 'bardic poetry', written almost to order by a multitude of poets before the war had really got going. As a poem of this date, Brooke's is head and shoulders above most of the others, and he sets a model which most of the later poets felt bound to reply to whether by imitation, parody or deliberate change of style. The patriotic sonnet, written in exalted language, was launched, almost like a projectile. Others had to make up their minds whether to reply to the challenge by matching like with like.

Brooke may be excused much in that he had seen little action, though he was involved for a short time in the evacuation of Antwerp. Generally Brooke's values were admired, but among the more intelligent of the poets they were soon rejected, especially by those who were involved in trench warfare. Charles Hamilton Sorley (see biographical entry) said in a letter of 28 April 1915:

I saw Rupert Brooke's death in *The Morning Post. The Morning Post,* which has always hitherto disapproved of him, is now loud in his praises because he has conformed to their stupid axiom of literary criticism that the only stuff of poetry is violent physical experience, by dying on active service. I think Brooke's earlier poems – especially notably *The Fish* and *Grantchester,* which you can find in *Georgian Poetry* – are his best. That last sonnet-sequence of his, of which you sent me the review in the *Times Lit. Sup.,* and which has been so praised, I find (with the exception of that beginning 'These hearts are woven of human joys and cares,/Washed marvellously with sorrow' which is not about himself) overpraised. He is far too obsessed with his own sacrifice, regarding the going to war of himself (and others) as a highly intense, remarkable and sacrificial exploit, whereas it is merely the conduct demanded of him (and others) by the turn of circumstances, where non-compliance with this demand would have made life intolerable.

Further to this, he wrote a poetic reply to Brooke, using the same form, though it actually uses a variation of the rhyme scheme of the Petrarchan sonnet:

> When you see millions of the mouthless dead
> Across your dreams in pale battalions go,
> Say not soft things as other men have said,
> That you'll remember. For you need not so.
> Give them not praise. For deaf, how should they know
> It is not curses heaped on each gashed head?
> Nor tears. The blind eyes see not your tears flow.
> Nor honour. It is easy to be dead.
> Say only this, 'They are dead.' Then add thereto,
> 'Yet many a better one has died before.'
> Then, scanning all the o'ercrowded mass, should you
> Perceive one face that you loved heretofore,
> It is a spook. None wears the face you knew.
> Great death has made all his for evermore.

In line 10 there is a reference to *Iliad,* XXI.106–7, where Achilles is speaking:

> So, friend, you must die too. Why do you whinge so much
>   about it?
> Even Patroklos is dead, a much better man than you are.

Sorley has rejected the abstract nouns which served to keep Brooke cheerful. The only exception, I suppose, is 'great death', but then he had been studying in Germany, where images of Death have a powerful presence in the culture.

Sorley was killed in 1915. We know that Owen had heard of Sorley because he made a note of the title of his posthumous volume of poetry on a piece of paper which was later used for a poem and this helps us to date the manuscript. He also owned copies of books by two poets who were much older than most of their fellow-soldiers. R.E. Vernède had volunteered to serve in 1914 although he was in his late thirties; he generally seems to reassure his readers with correct patriotic values, but some poems are uncomfortable. For example, 'Listening Post' is a story about two British snipers waiting 'to shoot the first man that goes by'. One of them tries to justify the action in prospect, because otherwise 'The world may lie in chains for years'. While thinking on these matters they hear a blackbird, who seems to be an innocent, and who doesn't know 'the world's askew':

> Strange that this bird sits there and sings
> While we must only sit and plan –
> Who are so much the higher things –
> The murder of our fellow man . . .

The ellipsis indicates that things have got too difficult for the soldier, and presumably for the poet, since the rest of the poem invokes God and then dissolves into empty moralising. But it is interesting in its vague Wordsworthian reverence for the voice of the natural world, and the use of the word 'murder' hovers on the edge of protest.

The other older poet was W.W. Gibson, who attempted to represent the experience of the common soldier. Here is his poem 'Breakfast':

> We ate our breakfast lying on our backs
> Because the shells were screeching overhead.
> I bet a rasher to a loaf of bread
> That Hull United would beat Halifax
> When Jimmy Stainthorpe played full-back instead
> Of Billy Bradford. Ginger raised his head
> And cursed, and took the bet, and dropt back dead.
> We ate our breakfast lying on our backs
> Because the shells were screeching overhead.

This might have been patronising but is in fact quite successful, and once again shows the use of the telling anecdote; this time it is employed without comment, anticipating the methods of Sassoon. In fact it was probably on Sassoon's recommendation that Wilfred Owen placed both these poets on his reading list for December 1917; it could therefore be said that Owen came to these two poets rather later in the war than we might expect.

On the same list he put the book of a much more popular poet, *Ardours and Endurances* by Robert Nichols. Nichols was in the Somme battle but was invalided out with shell-shock after August 1916. He specialised in snap-shots of trench life and sometimes attempted to imitate – in fluent experimental verse – the staccato experiences of battle. This is from 'The Assault':

> I hear my whistle shriek,
> Between teeth set;
> I fling an arm up,
> Scramble up the grime
> Over the parapet!
> I'm up. Go on.
> Something meets us.
> Head down into the storm that greets us.
> A wail.
> Lights. Blurr.
> Gone.
> On, on. Lead. Lead. Hail.
> Spatter. Whirr! Whirr!

Nichols's work has not worn well, though it may have seemed sensational at the time. Critics saw self-indulgence rather than protest here. Owen seems to have shared this view because he describes Nichols as 'so self-concerned and *vaniteux* in his verse' (*CL* p. 511). This impression must have filtered through to Robert Graves, who wrote to reassure Owen that 'Robert is a ripping fellow really but any stupid person would easily mistake him for an insufferable bounder' (*CL* p. 596). Another feature of his volume is that the second half consists of 'A Faun's Holiday' and various 'Phantasies' of an aesthetic kind; he continued to work on these simultaneously with his war poems. This provides a parallel to Wilfred Owen, who is often reproached for the minor verse on erotic and Wildean themes which he wrote alongside his more famous poems; some editions of Owen place the minor verse at the back of the volume so that it fortuitously resembles *Ardours and Endurances.*

After 1916 and the Somme battle there is a sharp division in the poets' attitude to the war. Sassoon, Graves and Blunden move in their different ways into an oppositional position, as far as that could be shown against the background of war propaganda, and their own self-censorship. Sassoon, who had begun with poems just as 'bardic' as others in the early stages of the war, had now developed the sarcasm and the edge which distinguish his most famous poems. For example, his feelings about the costly battles of the Somme and elsewhere are immortalised in 'The General':

> 'Good-morning; good-morning!' the General said
> When we met him last week on our way to the line.
> Now the soldiers he smiled at are most of 'em dead,
> And we're cursing his staff for incompetent swine.

'He's a cheery old card,' grunted Harry to Jack
As they slogged up to Arras with rifle and pack.

*

But he did for them both by his plan of attack.

Owen had bought Sassoon's 1917 volume *The Old Huntsman and Other Poems* before their meeting at Craiglockhart; he asked Sassoon to sign it in August 1917. As has been previously explained (see p. 25) Sassoon and Owen met regularly at this time; the influence of the older poet upon the younger was overwhelming and the culmination was the 'Anthem for Doomed Youth'. It is to be read here as the third sonnet in the Brooke/Sorley argument, which has already been presented in this chapter:

What passing-bells for these who die as cattle?
  Only the monstrous anger of the guns.
  Only the stuttering rifles' rapid rattle
Can patter out their hasty orisons.
No mockeries now for them; no prayers nor bells,
  Nor any voice of mourning save the choirs, –
The shrill, demented choirs of wailing shells;
  And bugles calling for them from sad shires.
What candles may be held to speed them all?
  Not in the hands of boys, but in their eyes
Shall shine the holy glimmers of good-byes.
  The pallor of girls' brows shall be their pall;
Their flowers the tenderness of patient minds,
And each slow dusk a drawing-down of blinds.

If Brooke is seen as rhetorical and Sorley as the opposite, Owen in some sense provides a synthesis here, supplying the theme of 'The Dead' with his own kind of Keatsian resonance, but also answering Brooke in the high style which the sonnet form seems to demand. The references to religious ceremonies, though they are all negated by the sense of the poem, remain as telling images in the mind, and the forceful rhythms of the verse serve to give back to the dead their due solemnities.

Similar points were being made by the others at roughly the same time, though the dating of individual poems can be difficult to establish. In 'Concert Party: Busseboom', Edmund Blunden describes an occasion, some way behind the lines, where a famous troop of actors have made everybody laugh; coming out of the hall they are aware of a different kind of theatricals:

We heard another matinée
  We heard the maniac blast
Of barrage

and concludes the poem with

> To this new concert, white we stood;
>   Cold certainty held our breath;
> While men in the tunnels below Larch Wood
>   Were kicking men to death

– an intensification of Wordsworth's melancholy at

> What man has done to man.

Blunden can get away with this because of the quietness of his tone, and the baffled innocence which shapes his ironies. Such truth-telling was rare however; the general run of poetry continued to exhibit evasions and half-truths.

There is of course no question of any influence here, because Owen would not have been able to read Blunden, who was published after the war; we have now reached the point where Owen has begun to speak out and other poets are working in parallel. Graves, on the other hand, he knew; he admired and corresponded with him. Though Owen ordered several copies of *Fairies and Fusiliers* in November 1917 (*CL* p. 506), it is very difficult to see that the volume had any direct influence on his work, partly because it came too late, and partly because Graves did not give reign to open criticism while the war was still in progress. His injunction to Owen:

> For God's sake cheer up and write more optimistically – The war's not ended yet but a poet should have a spirit above wars[5]

has often been quoted but is in fact totally out of tune with what Owen had been learning from Sassoon.

Notes

1   I am trying to make a general point of cultural history, and realise that these two authors would hardly have been known to our poets at the time. Though Joyce had published some early work, a volume of Hopkins was not available until 1918; Robert Bridges had included six poems in *The Spirit of Man*, a well-known anthology published in 1916.
2   Walter Pater, *The Renaissance*, 6th edn (London: Macmillan, 1901), p. 237.
3   In *Henley and South Oxfordshire Standard*, 2 October 1914.
4   In *The Spectator*, 8 August 1914.
5   Letter of December 1917, printed in *CL* p. 596.

8 The peace party and Siegfried Sassoon

As he lay in hospital in May 1917 recovering from a wound, Sassoon was so incensed by the lies then circulating that he felt he had a mission to expose the truth about the war. At this time he seems to have read a book by Bertrand Russell, probably *Principles of Social Reconstruction*. Russell was now a leading light in the peace movement; the organisation which he represented was the No-Conscription Fellowship. This had been founded by Fenner Brockway back in November 1914, bringing together Christians and Socialists, and was originally intended as a way of linking together young men of military age who were not willing to serve in the armed forces. When conscription was introduced in early 1916 the practical task of the Fellowship was to help the first wave of conscientious objectors who were being badly treated; but Russell was more interested in trying to stop the war. He was an indefatigable writer and propagandist, and in June 1916 he was put on trial because of his authorship of an 'undesirable pamphlet'. As a result of the trial his movements were restricted and he lost his fellowship at Trinity College, Cambridge.

In June 1917, when Sassoon had recovered sufficiently from his wound, he got in touch with Russell who helped him to decide on a course of action. As he had already served in the trenches he could hardly qualify as a conscientious objector, but it was decided that a public statement might lead to a court-martial with the appropriate publicity. In Part Ten of *Memoirs of an Infantry Officer*, Sassoon describes how everything came together in his mind. In spite of his different background, he was now broadly in sympathy with the aims of the peace party, who wished to bring the war to a close with a simple return of territory. He was also influenced by a magazine editor who told him that 'our Aims were essentially acquisitive' and 'what we were fighting for was the Mesopotamian Oil Wells'. He felt that he could no longer take part in such a war, and wrote out a statement which sought to show that the conflict was being prolonged unnecessarily.

> I am making this statement as an act of wilful defiance of military authority, because I believe that the War is being deliberately prolonged by those who have the power to end it. I am a soldier, convinced that I am acting on behalf of soldiers. I believe that this War, upon which I entered as a war of defence and liberation, has now become a war of aggression and conquest. I believe that the purposes for which I and my fellow soldiers entered upon this

War should have been so clearly stated as to have made it impossible to change them, and that, had this been done, the objects
which actuated us would now be obtainable by negotiation. I have
seen and endured the sufferings of the troops, and I can no longer
be a party to prolong these sufferings for ends which I believe to
be evil and unjust. I am not protesting against the conduct of the
War, but against the political errors and insincerities for which the
fighting men are being sacrificed. On behalf of those who are
suffering now I make this protest against the deception which is
being practised on them; also I believe that I may help to destroy
the callous complacency with which the majority of those at home
regard the continuance of agonies which they do not share, and
which they have not sufficient imagination to realize.[1]

Such remarks, when made public, could only be construed as treas-
onable, and possibly worthy of a prison sentence in the case of a
military officer. However, he was not at first proceeded against in
any way but simply left alone. It was decided that he must be suffering from shell-shock, and it was necessary for Robert Graves to
testify before a medical tribunal that Sassoon was off his head.

I applied for permission to give evidence as a friend of the patient.
There were three doctors on the board – a regular R.A.M.C.
colonel and major, and a captain, who was obviously a 'duration
of the war' man. I had not been long in the room when I realised
that the colonel was patriotic and unsympathetic, that the major
was reasonable but ignorant, and that the captain was a nerve-
specialist, right-minded, and my only hope. I had to go through
the whole story again. I was most deferential to the colonel and
major, but used the captain as an ally to break down their scruples.
I had to appear in the rôle of a patriot distressed by the mental
collapse of a brother-in-arms, a collapse directly due to his magnifi-
cent exploits in the trenches. I mentioned Siegfried's 'hallucinations' in the matter of corpses in Piccadilly. The irony of having to
argue to these mad old men that Siegfried was not sane! It was a
betrayal of the truth, but I was jesuitical. I was in nearly as bad a
state of nerves as Siegfried myself and burst into tears three times
in the course of my statement. Captain McDowall, whom I learned
later to be a well-known morbid psychologist, played up well and
the colonel was at last persuaded. As I went out he said to me:
'Young man, you ought to be before this board yourself.'[2]

By the time Sassoon arrived at Craiglockhart he was already
beginning to feel that his actions could be misinterpreted, and that
perhaps he had deserted his comrades. He continued to write during
his time in the hospital, and a poem such as the following shows the

embodiment of this guilt in its references to the terrors of the night: one has to understand that the dead really would feature in the hallucinations of a shell-shocked patient, and as with other visions suffered by Sassoon and Wilfred Owen, they are not simply a figure of speech or part of the 'poetry'.

'Sick Leave' – also known as 'Death's Brotherhood'

When I'm asleep, dreaming and drowsed and warm,
They come, the homeless ones, the noiseless dead.
While the dim charging breakers of the storm
Rumble and drone and bellow overhead,
Out of the gloom they gather about my bed.
They whisper to my heart; their thoughts are mine.

'Why are you here with all your watches ended?
From Ypres to Frise we sought you in the Line.'
In bitter safety I awake, unfriended;
And while the dawn begins with slashing rain
I think of the battalion in the mud.
'When are you going back to them again?
Are they not still your brothers through our blood?'

These matters must have been discussed with Owen, time and again.

Notes

1   Siegfried Sassoon, *Memoirs of an Infantry Officeer* (London: Faber and Faber, 1965), p. 218.
2   Robert Graves, *Goodbye to All That* (London: Cape, 1931), pp. 324–5.

9 Owen's mature position about the war

Was Wilfred Owen a pacifist? Certainly he made plenty of anti-war remarks and these antedate his meeting with Siegfried Sassoon, but they are in letters home and were not published openly. Also it is difficult at first to sort out conventional feelings of a longing for peace and statements that are noticeably unmilitary. For example, in his first letter from France in 1917 he says: 'There is a fine heroic feeling about being in France, and I am in perfect spirits' (*CL* p. 421), which is fair enough as an old-fashioned sentiment. After he has met his regiment and begun on the usual chores, his second letter comments: 'I censored hundreds of letters yesterday, and the hope of peace was in every one' (*CL* p. 422). This is of no importance but helps to establish a climate of feeling, which Owen seems to share.

After being sent back from the line with shell-shock, his letters begin to get incoherent – in my opinion – from about 14 May. This may simply be that he has nothing to tell and wishes to make jokes with a medley of Bible verses. Or it may be that the effect of the treatment at the hospital was beginning to tell. The next letter to his mother is certainly odd, yet it is here that the first wave of remarkable statements occur. He explains to his mother that the Christian education he had received is beginning to make him ask questions:

> Incidentally, I think the big number of texts which jogged up in my mind in half-an-hour bears witness to a goodly store of them in my being. It is indeed so; and I am more and more Christian as I walk the unchristian ways of Christendom. Already I have comprehended a light which never will filter into the dogma of any national church: namely that one of Christ's essential commands was: Passivity at any price! Suffer dishonour and disgrace; but never resort to arms. Be bullied, be outraged, be killed; but do not kill. It may be a chimerical and an ignominious principle, but there it is. . . .
>
> And am I not myself a conscientious objector with a very seared conscience? (*CL* p. 461)

He also amended the misused text which was discussed in Chapter 4 so that it reads:

> Greater love hath no man than this, that a man lay down his life – for a friend.
>
> Is it spoken only in English and French?

> I do not believe so.
>
> Thus you see how pure Christianity will not fit in with pure patriotism. (*CL* p. 461)

Two letters later on 23 May he reveals that he has recently had a temperature of 102.9, and has been incubating trench fever for some time past. All this may serve to provide a conventional 'he-didn't-really-mean-it' explanation of the revelations in the letter, but equally one can argue that the disease liberated thoughts which had been 'incubating' in his mind and released them from the usual self-censorship.

After Owen met Sassoon and came under his influence, he seems to have gone along with Sassoon's analysis of the war-situation and with many of his ideas. Both poets were 'cured' of neurasthenia and returned to the front. On 13 July 1918 Sassoon was mistakenly shot in the head by one of his own soldiers, and sent home. On 31 August Owen crossed to France, and quoted a recent poem of Sassoon's to his mother which begins:

> For the last time I say War is not glorious . . .

and continues

> I say we fight
> Because men lost their landmarks in the night . . .

This is not really much of an advance on the position taken by Sorley in 1915 in his sonnet 'To Germany':

> You are blind like us . . .

Sassoon's poem, which is really addressed to himself, concludes:

> O my heart,
> Be still; you have cried your cry, you have played your part!

and Owen, who repeats this cry in the same letter (*CL* p. 570), would seem at this point to share in this feeling of finality. On the same day he writes to Sassoon that he is nearer to him in France than in Scarborough, which may be literally true in geographical terms, but he also expressed the view that the real England had fled to France: 'Everything is clear now: and I am in hasty retreat towards the Front' (*CL* p. 571). When he eventually took part in a battle, and had won the Military Cross, he tells his mother: 'I came out in order to help these boys – directly by leading them as well as an officer can; indirectly, by watching their sufferings that I may speak of them as well as a pleader can. I have done the first' (*CL* p. 580). He is soon sending Sassoon a copy of the special Order of the day, which included the words: 'Peace talk in any form is to cease in Fourth Army. All ranks are warned against the disturbing influence of dangerous peace talk' (*CL* p. 583). His last letter, after describing the domestic details of the cellar where he is staying, radiates serenity:

> It is a great life. I am more oblivious than alas! yourself, dear Mother, of the ghastly glimmering of the guns outside, and the hollow crashing of the shells. . . . Of this I am certain you could not be visited by a band of friends half so fine as surround me here. (*CL* p. 591)

For further evidence of his state of mind at different times we shall have to consult the poems, remembering that here too there will be inconsistencies and difficulties of interpretation. We are not dealing with simple ideas; frequently the knotted-up complexity of the expression will mirror the complexity of the problems posed.

Part Three

Critical Survey

Critical survey of Owen's poetry

Yet these elegies are to this generation in no sense consolatory.
They may be to the next.

Unfinished preface to his poems

The art of Owen's poetry

Though Owen declared, bravely and almost casually with tongue in
cheek, in the same preface:

Above all I am not concerned with Poetry.
My subject is War, and the Pity of War.
The Poetry is in the pity.

in this short account of Owen's work I want to try to concentrate on
the poetry. This will not be easy as the poems appear to have other
aims. It will not be possible to disentangle the poetry from 'the pity'
or indeed from the other abstractions which Owen laboured to make
powerfully concrete. In the first instance I mean 'the truth', and yet
this seems to subdivide before our eyes into sincerity: 'true Poets
must be truthful' (Preface), and of course 'the truth untold' ('Strange
Meeting'). The first of these would seem to be a shield which deflects
any criticism, and the second something quite ineffable. Yet both
quotations in fact disclose the intention to inform the world of what
is still a secret. This brings us back to what can be discussed or
verified, the realism or better the war reporting aims of the poems as
messages, and secondly their effectiveness as instruments of persua-
sion. It is important then to recall that he called his major war
poems 'elegies', and to consider whether this genre would make any
demands upon truth in the name of pity.

Keeping these things in mind, the method adopted here will be to
pursue general topics, and from time to time to interweave detailed
discussion of individual poems.

The text and order of the poems

Ten poems are selected here to serve as an introduction to the poet's
work and for comment. These will be printed out in full, but for
others the reader will need to have recourse to a collection of the
poems, and will soon discover that there are variations between
editions. Editors like to establish a definitive version of a poem. Yet

in Wilfred Owen's case there are unusual difficulties because of the way in which his reading and experiences seem to have fermented into poetry and because of the nature of his working methods. In many cases he wrote his poems out again and again, which means, incidentally, that there are considerable problems about dating their initial composition (e.g. 'Exposure', see pp. 113–18). These constantly revised texts seem to be reaching their final form in the last year of his life, when he was thinking of preparing a volume for publication, but we do not really know if they are 'finished'. As one of the themes of this book is the way in which Owen was presented as a poet before and after his death, these poems have been arranged in order of publication. (This takes up the discussion started on p. 30.) Therefore the text used is, with one or two exceptions, that in which the poem first appeared in print.

Influences 1: Keats

The school of English poetry which Owen belongs to had derived from the Romantic poets at the beginning of the nineteenth century – writing should be personal (to the point of appearing confessional), sincere (which meant limitations on satire and humour), and richly loaded with imagery. What had seemed a new start at that time had become the norm after 1850; so that Gerard Manley Hopkins, who tried to break new ground, was to speak of a 'Parnassian style' as the high-flown but common means of poetic expression. (Although widely known now, his own poems were largely unheard of before 1918 as his work was not generally available.) Owen was introduced to the Romantics at school, but he does not seem to have encountered the later nineteenth-century poets in the same way. He heard of Wilde and Swinburne, for example, at a much later stage. Of all these poets it was Keats who seemed to provide a role model. There are the ironies (to us, with hindsight) of the almost exact parallels between the length of their lives, i.e. twenty-six years, and the fact that their important writing was crammed into one year; for both men, the large bulk of their writing which does survive consists of their letters.

The early poems written to Keats radiate hero-worship, e.g. 'Written in a Wood, September 1910' and 'On Seeing a Lock of Keats's Hair'. These are rather juvenile efforts, but the study of Keats did permanently influence Owen's choice of verse-forms; in particular he frequently attempted the sonnet, and sometimes the ode. Occasionally – it seems to me – the shorter descriptive poems are a form of the verse-letter. Owen's attempts at longer narrative are also indebted to Keats, e.g. 'Hercules and Antaeus', but are not really more than exercises.

But years of reading the earlier poet's work had familiarised Owen with the main features of Keats's special vocabulary, and his use of it in slow rhythmical effects. This led him to a choice of words which are long (in duration), dark rather than light in tone, but (negatively) sometimes seem too beautiful for the task ahead. This is difficult to illustrate without quotation from Keats; yet what we are really looking for is a continuation of his style after a hundred years and the validity of any suggestions must be a matter of opinion. For example, the way that Owen's sonnet 'Maundy Thursday' ends with

> I kissed the warm live hand that held the thing

may go back ultimately to Keats's

> This living hand, now warm and capable
> 'Lines supposed to have been addressed to Fanny Brawne'

or

> To let the warm Love in!
> 'Ode to Psyche'

but this does not tell us much that we could not foresee from any word-by-word close reading of Keats and Owen. Whereas the ending of the 'Anthem for Doomed Youth',

> And each slow dusk a drawing-down of blinds

one of the slowest lines to read aloud in the English language, owes everything to the discipline inculcated by Keats in his 'Sonnet on the Sonnet':

> . . . Let us inspect the Lyre, and weigh the stress
> Of every chord, and see what may be gain'd
> By ear industrious and attention meet;
> Misers of sound and syllable, no less
> Than Midas of his coinage, let us be
> Jealous of dead leaves in the bay wreath crown. . . .

First publications

Owen published some of his own poems in *The Hydra*, the magazine of Craiglockhart Hospital, while he was editor. Considering that this was an army hospital, with a sort of 'all boys together' atmosphere among the fitter patients, he would presumably be laughed at for anything too outré. We may be amazed to find that his first published poem was 'Song of Songs', though it was unsigned.

Song of Songs

Sing me at morn but only with your laugh;
Even as Spring that laugheth into leaf;
Even as Love that laugheth after Life.

Sing me but only with your speech all day,
As voluble leaflets do; let viols die;
The least word of your lips is melody!

Sing me at eve but only with your sigh!
Like lifting seas it solaceth; breathe so,
Slowly and low, the sense that no songs say.

Sing me at midnight with your murmurous heart!
Let youth's immortal-moaning chords be heard
Throbbing through you, and sobbing, unsubdued.

COMPOSITION One feels instinctively that this was laboured over for some time, but it may have been dashed off in August 1917; by now Owen was adept at this manner of writing. Another version of the poem exists with some alterations.

PUBLICATION This is the text as it appeared in *The Hydra* on 1 September 1917. But it also came to national attention as it was printed in *The Bookman* in May 1918 (in an altered version). This was one of the three winners in a competition. Owen was quite ashamed when it won a prize, and told his mother it was 'a mere idle joke, an old lyric I condescended to send from Scarboro'. It gained me only a book. The Bookman people are hopeless bad literary people' (*CL* p. 554). It was significantly excluded from the posthumous volume edited by Sassoon.

THE SENSE OF THE POEM Does it matter? The title from *The Song of Solomon* must surely prefigure a love poem. At a first reading it seems somewhat nonsensical, if we take it literally; 'sing but don't sing' would seem to be all that is said. In fact, looked at carefully, one can see a fourfold pattern of the times of day and night, careful variations within each stanza, and a gathering intensity of emotion. When one gets to the midnight 'throbbing' – a very amorous word in Keats – it is tempting to say that this is an erotic poem, which is reaching a climax in the fourth stanza; but I don't think that *The Bookman* or the general mass of its readers would have wanted to take it in this way. It is not therefore the subject matter but the 'music' of the poem which must have won the prize; the competition was for a lyric.

THE LYRIC Reading this poem one thinks of other lyrics from an earlier period, e.g. 'What the Thrush Said' by Keats, or the songs from Tennyson's medley, *The Princess*. Tennyson's influence will be discussed more fully in a moment, but the poems which come to mind here are 'Now sleeps the crimson petal, now the white' and 'O Swallow, Swallow'. In the first of these Tennyson does not rhyme at all, but every reader is satisfied with the poem as a carefully patterned song and not as a piece of blank verse. One near rhyme is to be found in the concluding lines (my italics):

> Now folds the lily all her sweetness *up*,
> And slips into the bosom of the lake:
> So fold thyself, my dearest, thou, and *slip*
> Into my bosom and be lost in me.

'O Swallow, Swallow' is in three-line stanzas which are completely unrhymed; here and there, however, the reader can find a hint of consonantal agreement. A stanza which might have influenced Owen is:

> O tell her brief is life but love is long,
> And brief the sun of summer in the North,
> And brief the moon of beauty in the South.

but it is arguable whether Tennyson would have thought he was using consonantal rhyme at the end of the last two lines.

CONSONANTAL OR HALF-RHYME Similarly, it is possible that the uninitiated reader of Owen's poem at the time it was written would have taken it at first to be in a kind of blank verse; see the review of 'Strange Meeting' quoted on p. 105. The line endings are, for the time, experimental and show Owen's familiarity with consonantal rhyming at this stage of his poetic career, a familiarity which may have come from studying French verse. Unlike the war poems, the device is being used for a 'sweet' effect and not to disconcert the reader.

COMMENT Because of what we think we know about the Great War, and because we assume that at the time everybody was only interested in war poems, there is something unexpectedly embarrassing to us about this poem as a product of mid-1917 – after battle experience. Day-Lewis, in his edition, commented that this was 'interesting as an example of Owen's relapse into the "poetic" manner of his juvenilia'.[1] Unfortunately this won't do; this was the way he was writing in mid-1917 so it isn't a 'lapse'. The truth is that this is one of the most advanced poems that Owen had written by that date; but apart from the consonantal rhyming, which is original to Owen, it is a late extension of the Victorian poetic tradition, and can hardly be said to have caught up with the Georgians. It goes without saying

that it was written before meeting Sassoon, and exemplifies the aims
of the school of Gunston and Joergens. But even this patronising
comment won't do because, as we have seen, there were also poems
like this at the back of Robert Nichols's volume. This helps to explain why in 1918 Wilfred Owen sent this poem – and not one of his
war poems – to *The Bookman*. In terms of public taste it was accept-
able; it represented what 'poetry' meant at the time, and helps us to
understand what Owen meant in his Preface when he said 'I am not
concerned with Poetry'.

CONCLUSION Sassoon's influence will be discussed later, but a note is
necessary here. When it was shown to him amongst a welter of 'old
sonnets', Sassoon picked it out, and pronounced it 'perfect work,
absolutely charming, etc. etc.' (*CL* p. 486). The way Owen tells the
story to Gunston in this letter shows that he could hardly believe his
ears, yet that he was conscious that Sassoon might simply have been
humouring him. He did not send the poem to Gunston. One of the
more awful ironies is that the last stanza speaks of 'your murmurous
heart'. Leslie was excluded from military service with a 'heart murmur', and I cannot believe that the verbally conscious Owen would
have missed this appalling pun at second reading.

Owen's first publication in an important national magazine was
'Miners'. *The Nation* was a weekly journal sympathetic to advanced
ideas and in particular to the aims of the 'peace group'.

Miners

There was a whispering in my hearth,
  A sigh of the coal,
Grown wistful of a former earth
  It might recall.

I listened for a tale of leaves
  And smothered ferns,
Frond-forests, and the low sly lives
  Before the fawns.

My fire might show steam-phantoms simmer
  From Time's old cauldron,
Before the birds made nests in summer,
  Or men had children.

But the coals were murmuring of their mine,
  And moans down there
Of boys that slept wry sleep, and men
  Writhing for air.

I saw white bones in the cinder-shard,
　Bones without number.
For many hearts with coal are charred,
　And few remember.

I thought of all that worked dark pits
　Of war, and died
Digging the rock where Death reputes
　Peace lies indeed:

Comforted years will sit soft-chaired,
　In rooms of amber,
The years will stretch their hands, well-cheered
　By our life's ember;

The centuries will burn rich loads
　With which we groaned,
Whose warmth shall lull their dreaming lids,
　While songs are crooned;
But they will not dream of us poor lads
　Lost in the ground.

COMPOSITION It is usually assumed that the work was occasioned by the Halmerende pit disaster which had been in the news, but there had been many such events in recent times. This poem seems to have been written quite rapidly – 'half-hour's work' (*CL* p. 531). But it does not feel like a poem about a shocking disaster of one or two days ago; the miners who died then are not referred to in the title and it could be said that justice is not really done to them in this poem. In addition, such rapid publication is not like *The Nation*, which took time over his later contributions. Furthermore, it has sometimes been assumed to have been the poem mentioned in a letter of 10 November 1917 when Owen tells his mother that he has 'sent something to the *Nation* which hasn't appeared yet' (*CL* p. 507). It was possibly written at Craiglockhart, which would fit with Sassoon's being able to 'correct' it. It was accepted by *The Nation* some time before 10 November, judging by other remarks in the letter.

PUBLICATION Published in *The Nation* on 26 January 1918; this is the text used here, for which Owen had seen a proof (*CL* p. 527). Sassoon had seen the poem in draft and suggested alterations. (In his edition Jon Stallworthy has restored the original line 19, 'Many the muscled bodies charred', and the last line 'Left in the ground'.) Other editions, following Sassoon's 'improvements', print 'Lost in the ground' and this was, after all, what Owen published during his lifetime.

TITLE In one of his lists of contents for a proposed volume this poem is subtitled: 'How the Future will forget the dead in war'. In both lists this poem is placed first, and must be thought of in this position as a way into the elegiac mood.

CONSONANTAL RHYME AND ASSONANCE Owen announces himself to the world with a poem in consonantal rhyme (which links it back to 'Song of Songs' and shows that Owen was working with this new skill constantly at this time). The unsettling effect of this device must have been quite strong to a contemporary reader, judging by the reported comment of his friend Leslie Gunston, who said the rhymes in this poem offended his 'musical ear' (*CL* p. 530). Since the frequent use of this kind of rhyme by Auden and others, we are not likely to be so offended, though see further in the discussion under 'Exposure' (p. 118). Here it could be said to have a gentler enriching effect, which compels the attention that might not be given to full rhymes. Owen in fact felt the need to justify the poetic device in his reply to Leslie: 'I suppose I am doing in poetry what the advanced composers are doing in music. I am not satisfied with either' (*CL* p. 531). The set of feminine rhymes – 'number', 'remember', 'amber' and 'ember' – seem particularly successful. Others such as 'crooned' seem unfortunate, but the word has become debased since Owen's time. Critical discussion has also centred on whether the half-rhymes are leading the thought of the poem.

VOCABULARY The selection and the careful placing of the words are Keatsian: for example in the last two stanzas 'soft-chaired' (a typical Keatsian double adjective) and the 'rich loads' ('load every rift with ore'). These effects build to the 'amber glow' which seems to suffuse the room in this part of the poem. There are onomatopoeic effects too – in the noises from the fire at the beginning the 'whispering' is taken up by 'wistful' and there are further sibilants taking up the 's' and 'f' of this word in the next stanza. 'Smothered' may indeed seem a somewhat strong expression for ferns and may prepare us, as Jon Silkin suggests, for the smothered miners later in the poem. But there are tougher sources than Keats for some of the vocabulary. The tricky abstractions in the lines

> Digging the rock where Death reputes
> Peace lies indeed

hint at the false hopes of the seeker who will only obtain the 'peace' of death, a point emphasised by the double meaning in 'lies' as in 'Here lies . . .'. This kind of writing echoes the opening of Dr Johnson's well-known poem 'On the death of Dr Robert Levet':

Condemn'd to hope's delusive mine,
  As on we toil from day to day,
By sudden blasts, or slow decline,
  Our social comforts drop away.

Johnson, coming from Staffordshire, knew about mining, but obviously the point of resemblance here is the way in which hope is both an abstract good which we seek and also a delusion.

NARRATIVE METHOD The poet is indulging in reverie, brought on by dozing in front of the fire. The gentle noises of the first stanzas serve to lull the readers into this state too. If we were too wide-awake some features of the poem would be censored as being unjustified or impossible, for example the fire showing us all these scenes. Nor is our moral sense fully aware of the repercussions of what is being described. But this does not worry us at all, and we do not allow our 'prose-minds' to object. Reverie of course provides the background to many of the great Romantic meditative poems, e.g. Coleridge's 'Frost at Midnight' and Keats's 'Ode to a Nightingale' ('Do I wake or sleep?'), and is a method of entry to their dream-visions. Such poems are characterised by sudden shifts of mood and this poem has a similar dream-logic. This logic leads us from the geology to the coal-miners and then to the war; finally we encounter the images of the people of the future who have been comforted by the efforts of the lost lads.

FORM OF THE POEM The poem seems to offer itself as a ballad. It is worth asking why this form is chosen, or indeed whether it mismatches the thought of the poem. The ballad had many uses in the nineteenth century, but originally it was used to tell a disaster-story. Is this relevant here? In this case there is no story which drives the ballad-singer along, though of course the pit-disasters are 'understood'. In fact you could be very negative about the poem and say that as a narrative it is flawed by false starts and takes a long time to get to the point. There is confusion as the miners change into soldiers, though to be fair to the poet, as Douglas Kerr points out, he may have been thinking of the many members of the Manchester regiment who were miners in civilian life. (Tunnelling was a strategy frequently practised in the trenches in order to undermine or blow up the opposing front line, as did the great mine at Messines; such tunnels are alluded to in 'Strange Meeting'.) A ballad-singer would surely be more satirical about the comfortable visions of the last stanzas; ballads about sea-disasters frequently allude to the uncaring lack of understanding of those on shore. In this case the civilians at home in the future have been saved by the sacrifice of the soldiers.

The civilians could have been caricatured as pig-ignorant in their oblivion. In fact the gentle mood of this sleepy poem protects them (think of the sinister female figure with her 'wall of boys' in 'The Kind Ghosts', p. 121). Perhaps the best comparison is once again with Keats, in whose ballad of 'La Belle Dame sans Merci' the desolation of the closing stanzas anticipates the awful finality of Owen's 'Lost in the ground'.

EDUCATION AND SCIENCE There is a curiously educational feel to this poem, and it is worth recalling that Owen did give lectures on botany and geology in Edinburgh as part of his work-therapy. He also did some teaching in school, and would have known about object lessons where, for example, a lump of coal might be placed in front of the children. Welland points out that both coal and amber are similar fossil products. Of course 'Pictures in the Fire' is a classic school-essay title of the time.

The opening is also reminiscent of Wellsian science; in its expectations of the 'news' to be garnered from time-travelling, it resembles the Time Machine's journeys. There are visions of the remote past and the remote future. We encounter 'the low sly lives' of reptiles and lizards before meeting the mammals – the fawns. In the second half of the poem there is also an *underworld* of the hard-working miners and an *overworld* of the civilians which is exactly like the Morlocks and the Eloi. Putting all this back into the discussion of the poem is difficult but there is a sense of the progress of an argument in this text. The miners arrive at their final solution by an inevitable QED kind of demonstration. This leads us to think of the all-knowing position of the narrator.

POINT OF VIEW Logically one could say that the narrator is dead or immortal if the end of the poem is to be taken literally. Actually what happens is that the prophet-poet, released from time, anticipates his own death and tells of what will happen later. (Romantic poetry is full of prophecy so this does not bother us.) What is odd is that the dreaming soul also seems to speak to us from a point beyond death, *recalling* 'us poor lads/ Lost in the ground' – this is therefore one of the poems that adds to the oracular effect of Owen's most memorable poetry.

Influences 2: Tennyson

At the time when Owen was growing up, Tennyson was unavoidable. Victoria's most famous laureate seemed to be identified with the conservative values associated with his Queen, and therefore he had become an institutional figure, enshrined on the bookshelves of the middle classes. If, as in the famous words of *1066 and all that*, 'history came to a stop' at this period, so too with Tennyson, who represented perfection, poetry had come to a stop. In Owen's education, especially when you consider the time lag before recent texts become established in schools, he was a generally pervasive influence, inculcated through anthologies and the prevailing taste of teachers. In any case he is a good poet, and spent his life pursuing the identification of sound with sense; in this area you might say that Tennyson taught the younger poet all he knew.

Owen was therefore steeped in Tennyson and absorbed details of his life as well as his poetry from an early age. In a verse letter about Oxfordshire written in December 1911 (quoted in Blunden's *Memoir*, but now lost), he tells us that 'the marriage-psalm/ Was sung o'er Tennyson, small space away'.

In Owen's time at Dunsden, Tennyson was a continuing presence, judging from little clues in the letters. He is associated with leisure and gardens (*CL* p. 127), but Owen found he had to quickly improvise some Tennyson readings for the Mothers' Social Evening (*CL* p. 107). Tennyson was worshipped in the little circle that gathered round Leslie Gunston; in fact Gunston sent Owen a leatherbound copy of Tennyson's poems while he was in Bordeaux (*CL* p. 225). Tennyson was not dropped from Owen's reading after his enlistment and his library shows that he continued to collect early editions of Tennyson's poems in 1916 and 1917. Tennyson was famous for his attempts to use the latest discoveries of science in his poetry, and therefore provided illustrations for the botanical lectures which Owen gave in Edinburgh.

A great deal of stress may be laid upon Owen's most famous remarks about Tennyson, and certainly they are both scathing and exactly right for the time – with the Bloomsbury Group rejecting the Victorians wholesale. Owen had by now seen the battlefield and was recovering at Craiglockhart in August 1917:

> The other day I read a Biography of Tennyson, which says he was unhappy, even in the midst of his fame, wealth, and domestic serenity. Divine discontent! I can quite believe he never knew happiness for one moment such as I have – for one or two moments. But as for misery, was he ever frozen alive, with dead men for comforters. Did he hear the moaning at the bar, not at twilight and the evening bell only, but at dawn, noon, and night, eating and sleeping, walking and working, always the close moaning of the Bar; the thunder, the hissing and the whining of the Bar?
>
> _____
>
> Tennyson, it seems, was always a great child.
> So should I have been, but for Beaumont Hamel. (*CL* p. 482)

91

This reads like a young man's dismissive judgement upon a fallen idol. It also seems to present Owen as having progressed beyond Tennyson to the next stage of poetic life, because of the nature of his experiences. A few days later, while building up his courage to make himself known to Sassoon, he wrote to his mother: 'I think if I had the choice of making friends with Tennyson or with Sassoon I should go to Sassoon' (*CL* p. 485). In spite of this remark Owen still recommends *The Idylls* to her in February 1918.

More importantly he drew up a list of *Projects* on 5 May 1918 at Ripon:

1 To write blank-verse plays on old Welsh themes. Models: Tennyson, Yeats, 1920
2 Collected Poems. (1919)
3 Perseus.
4 Idylls in Prose. (*CL* p. 551)

The war poems, in this plan for the future, are to be published and done with. That vein is mined out. He sees himself returning to the real duties of a poet with verse-plays and other Tennysonian projects.

The next poem was published with 'Futility' in *The Nation* on 15 June 1918 with the following short title, though it is often called 'Hospital Barge at Cérisy'.

Hospital Barge

Budging the sluggard ripples of the Somme
A barge round old Cèrisy slowly slewed.
Softly her engines down the current screwed,
And chuckled softly with contented hum,
Till fairy tinklings struck their crooning dumb.
The waters rumpling at the stern subdued:
The lock-gate took her bulging amplitude:
Gently from out the gurgling lock she swum.

One reading by that calm bank shaded eyes
To watch her lessening westward quietly.
Then, as she neared the bend, her funnel screamed.
And that long lamentation made him wise
How unto Avilon in agony
Kings passed in the dark barge which Merlin dreamed.

NOTE ON THE TEXT There is a British Library MS of 8 December 1917, but the text printed here is a later version for which Owen presumably saw proofs, as he had done for 'Miners'. However, in line 2 the grave accent on Cerisy (though there is no accent on this name in maps of the area) might be an argument for saying that he had *not* seen them. 'Avilon' for MS 'Avalon' and Tennyson's 'Avilion' (see below) is equally a cause for worry – or a sublime conflation by Owen, giving him two matching triads of vowels in 'Avilon in agony'.

DATE OF COMPOSITION The poem seems to relate to the experiences referred to in a letter of 10 May 1917 when Wilfred was at the 13th Casualty Clearing Station.

> I sailed in a steam-tug about 6 miles down the Canal with another 'inmate'.
>
> The heat of the afternoon was Augustan; and it has probably added another year to my old age to have been able to escape marching in equipment under such a sun.
>
> The scenery was such as I never saw or dreamed of since I read the *Fairie Queene*. Just as in the Winter when I woke up lying on the burning cold snow I fancied I must have died & been pitch-forked into the Wrong Place, so, yesterday, it was not more difficult to imagine that my dusky barge was wending up to Avalon, and the peace of Arthur, and where Lancelot heals him of his grievous wound. (*CL* p. 457)

It must therefore have been written after that date, but before 8 December. In fact it is usually dated to December, and is a good example of a Wordsworthian 'recollection in tranquillity'. Yet as with Wordsworth, who often made similar changes to the 'biographical reality', it is not simply a literal report of the incident described in the letter since the consciousness of the narrator is firmly located on the bank and not on board the ship. It is little details like this that betray the fictive element in the making of poetry.

VOCABULARY Considering that the poem narrates the slow progress of a barge down a canal and into a lock, the words used are often very lively. In particular some of the verbs and the adjectives formed from verbs are pushing and shoving their way into the quieter general mood (represented by 'softly', 'gently' and 'hum') in a rather vulgar manner, you might say. Look at 'Budging' and 'slewed'; I also include 'rumpling', 'bulging' and 'gurgling', though these also suggest the actions of an overgrown person. Douglas Kerr goes beyond this and says quite boldly that the barge is compared to a fat woman: 'the matronly "Hospital Barge" with her soft crooning voice, her gentle movements, and "bulging amplitude" ' (Kerr p. 59). Keats would surely have liked these mimetic usages; Tennyson, who in any case provides the subtext to the poem, would have admired the musical progress of the poem as a whole.

ASSONANCE If you read the poem aloud and listen to the words listed
above for sound rather than sense you may have noticed that the
first section of the poem is full of short-winded stumpy syllables like
'budge' and 'slug', which come back with variations in 'bulge' and
'gurgle'. 'Ripple' and 'rumple', 'chuck' and 'struck' are other pairs;
in nearly all these cases the first syllable has a short vowel-sound and
is end-stopped with double or triple consonants. These hobble or
constrict the voice from singing out, though there is a sweeter melody
in the quiet background. In the last six lines longer vowels come into
play, so that the forceful irruption of 'screamed' is totally unexpected. The last three lines resolve this into a richer music; all the
words in the penultimate line begin with vowels (if we include 'h'),
and end with vowels or 'n' so that they are like an Italian phrase.
The mouth can be opened and the words sung; finally the three
matching vowels in 'passed', 'dark' and 'barge' call for a deeper note
for the voice. While this kind of analysis can easily be faulted (the
shade of Edith Sitwell hovers in dire warning), the check is to be
found when we work at the meaning and see it developing into a
similar pattern. There is the sense here of Owen trying things out
and finally mastering his own style.

A DISCORDANT NOTE In line 5 the 'fairy tinklings' might seem weak if
not inappropriate. One respects D.S.R. Welland's objections (Welland
pp. 76–7). What Owen seems to mean is that the deeper noises of
the engines are replaced by the clinking noises of lock-machinery and
chains; heard at a distance these are subdued to 'tinklings'. The word
'fairy' may be a joke, or perhaps a reference to Ariel's music in *The
Tempest* – 'Full fathom Five'. Here it works as a Romantic signal, and
heralds the 'supernatural' ending to the poem, so that this is not an
unsuspected jolt when it comes upon us. Also lines 4 and 5, taken together, are a parodic recollection of some famous lines in a Keats sonnet:

> Hear ye not the hum
> Of mighty workings? –
> Listen awhile, ye nations, and be dumb.
> 'Sonnet to B.R. Haydon'

NARRATIVE WITHIN THE SONNET FORM There has been some discussion about what the barge is actually doing. In the first eight lines,
the octet of the sonnet, a sequence of events is described so that we
follow the leisurely movements of the boat in and out of the lock and
down the canal. According to tradition, the sonnet then turns at the
ninth line to what seems a new subject but is in fact a reflection
upon the first part of the poem. We now approach the meaning of
what we have seen.

As in many other Great War poems, a scene of the present war is set against old romance (see Asquith, p. 64). The references are to Tennyson's 'Morte D'Arthur', which he re-used and amplified as 'The Passing of Arthur' in *The Idylls of the King*. Although the poem is well-known, it is worth recalling because Owen has some close points of reference. After the last battle in the West the wounded King is taken off in 'a dusky barge' by the three queens; the scene is 'like a dream', and their cry is 'an agony/Of lamentation'. Sir Bedivere sees the barge depart, he is told, 'to the island-valley of Avilion'; he strains to watch it fading in the distance till it becomes a dot upon the mere. So, in Owen's sonnet, our barge is 'lessening westward'. In fact, the King's final destiny is deliberately obscured in Tennyson's poem. Merlin had prophesied in 'The Coming of Arthur': 'From the great deep to the great deep he goes'. In Owen's poem the concluding words – 'which Merlin dreamed' – seem to convey a lot more than the fact that Merlin the wizard invented the barge, and the line could be read to mean that he dreamed the whole story.

CONCLUSION Irony is produced here by the clash of two kinds of discourse. It is like using archaic equipment to measure and describe a contemporary setting; at first the narrator cannot quite see the meaning of what he is watching, though 'fairy tinklings' hint at an attempt to see through the appearances of the present. The barge, which is described realistically up to a point, would not be thought of as having such a heroic dimension at all, except by an exceptional spectator ('One'); and in the words 'made him wise' the narrator tells us that the experience enabled that spectator to understand the 'agony' in Tennyson's 'Morte D'Arthur', which he might previously have thought of as entertainment only, a poetic fantasy or a 'dream'. Now he realises that Tennyson did try to describe war and the destiny of wounded men, and the magnanimity of the earlier poet is called in to help us understand the deeper meaning of what we are witnessing now. This is a hospital ship, but at first we had laughed at it as a dumpy old barge and had not thought of the wounded and their agony. This the reference to Romantic poetry supplies: 'The poetry is in the pity' sometimes, but here the pity is in the 'poetry'.

Futility

Move him into the sun –
Gently its touch awoke him once,
At home, whispering of fields half-sown.
Always it woke him, even in France,
Until this morning and this snow.
If anything might rouse him now
The kind old sun will know.

Think how it wakes the seeds –
Woke once the clays of a cold star.
Are limbs, so dear-achieved, are sides
Full-nerved, still warm, too hard to stir?
Was it for this the clay grew tall?
– O what made fatuous sunbeams toil
To break earth's sleep at all?

COMPOSITION The poem is presumably early to mid 1918. There are various drafts which do illuminate the progress of the poem; in particular the strong ending seems to have been arrived at quite late in the sequence.

PUBLICATION The date of first publication is 15 June 1918 in *The Nation,* where it appeared with the previous poem 'Hospital Barge'. This is the text reproduced here.

THE STORY Surely this is a general statement about war and does not need to refer to a specific incident. Those wishing to pursue a very literal reading of the poem may follow those commentators who say that it seems to recall an incident in the snow at the battle of St Quentin. But this is unnecessary if not misleading because the snow is part of the symbolic structure, almost allegory, behind the poem.

ANOTHER ELEGY? In Wilfred Owen's lists of poems for publication, 'Futility' is placed next to 'Hospital Barge'. The descriptive subheading for both poems is 'Grief'. It is significantly not classed as a 'Protest' poem at all, but the classification of the poem is important to establish the way in which we read it – sonorously with tears, or spitting it out as a crying shame. In his edition Jon Silkin says it 'hovers between outrage and elegy' (p. 84).

The relation to classical elegy needs exploring. Owen had been reading Bion and Moschus, as well as Milton's *Lycidas* and Shelley's *Adonais* which derive in part from these classical originals. There is no Christianity in this elegy; admittedly there had not been any overt Christianity in the previous two poems, but the fact that the miners' lives are a sacrifice to the future, and that 'Hospital Barge' hints at the Arthurian otherworld, do give us a crumb of hope. In this poem death is final, there is nothing else; this is one of the factors which makes classical tragedy, e.g. the *Antigone* of Sophocles, so hard to accommodate to a Christian upbringing.

IMAGES Running behind the poem is the natural cycle of plant life. The snow is too cold for life; the sun will warm the earth, seeds will generate. The crops are to be sown, and they grow tall. In this context death is unthinkable, but the word 'half-sown' has a sting in it. The labourer has not completed his work in the fields; in metaphorical terms his life is only half-lived.

Once again the poem has the H.G. Wells's version of science and geology in it. The whole process of evolution from the beginnings of life on earth has led to this moment. When man stood up, the clay grew tall. Similarly Progress had led us to this point in time; now, as in *Clio and the Children*, there is blood on the pages of history. This point was anticipated in Tennyson's *In Memoriam*, where the poet tries to come to terms with the death of his friend. Tennyson's frequent use of natural imagery and geological explanation were familiar to Owen. Owen might well have picked up an approach, a mood, from such sections as LXVIII

> I dream'd there would be Spring no more

or CXVII

> They say,
> The solid earth whereon we tread
> In tracts of fluent heat began,
> And grew to seeming-random forms,
> The seeming prey of cyclic storms,
> Till at the last arose the man . . .

Commentators have pointed to section LV, which contains the word 'futile', but would Owen really need Tennyson to teach him the use of this word, which, in its longer noun form, seems very modern here?

VOCABULARY Coming after the Latin resonance of the title, the monosyllabic English words are those which a soldier would understand, and communication at this level had become very important to Owen; most lines have only one word that is longer than one syllable, and the most effective are monosyllabic throughout:

> The kind old sun will know

> Think how it wakes the seeds

> Was it for this the clay grew tall?

Compare the poem 'Asleep', which has roughly the same subject matter, to see Owen employing his usual rich vocabulary, here represented only by 'dear-achieved' and 'full-nerved'. In this context we should approach the description of 'the kind old sun' which some have seen as childish, sentimental or almost 'nursery rhyme' in its choice of words. The sun is treated as a genial uncle or a fond parent; the geological history informs us that it literally *is* in the second stanza. The words also connect back to 'home' in line 3, the early years when he was passive and had to be moved by others, and are appropriate to his father's or his mother's voice. To a soldier in winter the sun is sometimes the only source of warmth anyway, and in 'Spring Offensive' the sun is 'like a friend'. The word 'France' in the fourth line is bang up to date in its modernity of reference, yet ominous to those who know what 'France' now means. In the same phrase the word 'even' includes an ironical joke in that he slept through the noise which would keep others awake, yet was still, as a former agriculturalist, woken by the sun.

However, there are some words which seem to be less modern and familiar; both 'clay', instead of soil or earth, and 'star', to describe a planet, in this case the earth, are eighteenth-century or possibly Shelleyan in their usage.

HALF-RHYME Most of the lines are quite heavily end-stopped and the half-rhymes are very close to what we would normally expect from full rhymes; and so they do not trigger unease as in 'Exposure'. The poet cleverly conceals that he is using his new device of consonantal rhyming because the concluding lines of each stanza contain a traditional full rhyme which would normally emphasise closure. This mixture of the two different rhyming skills is completed and yet broken in the ending of the second stanza. Here 'tall' and 'at all' are using both systems at once. This is over the top and becomes discordant. The pathos in 'at all' is brilliantly conveyed in the sung version in Benjamin Britten's *War Requiem*.

CONCLUSION The poem is a forceful rebuttal of the nineteenth-century view of the meaning of human life. We have come a long journey from Tennyson's *In Memoriam*, and also from the traditional ways in which poems were classified and kept under gentlemanly control. The whole structure of the work builds from a quiet mood towards 'fatuous', which is not an elegiac word but a satirical word, as if the poet has lost control of the genre he is working in. It is Modernist in its dislocation of the reader's expectations: we expect an elegy yet we get a protest instead of the traditional ending.

Influences 3: Shelley

Although the study of the language of Keats and Tennyson had provided Owen with the foundations of his poetic vocabulary and his highly self-conscious technique, it was in the work of Shelley that he first encountered challenging ideas. Where Keats and Tennyson had supplied sweetness, Shelley gave out light.

Owen had known about Shelley from an early stage of his reading – at school and elsewhere. He went on to read lives of the poet and critical works. These may have conditioned his initial responses to the poet, for Victorian interpreters found themselves under pressure to edit out the revolutionary aspects of their subject; they could not deal with somebody as far to the left as this in politics, or so 'free' in his attitude to love, and therefore presented a bowdlerised version of Shelley to their reading public. He became more or less than human – the famous 'ineffectual angel'. But this view never survives an extensive study of Shelley's life and poetry, and this Wilfred was prepared to put his mind to.

This investment of time and energy paid its dividend at Dunsden. When Owen read *Shelley* by John Addington Symonds, he discovered that his hero had lived nearby:

> I find that Shelley lived at a cottage within easy cycling distance from here. And I was very surprised (tho' really I don't know why) to find that he used to 'visit the sick in their beds; kept a regular list of the industrious poor whom he assisted to make up their accounts;' and for a time walked the hospitals in order to be more useful to the poor he visited. (*CL* p. 106)

The vicar would have been shocked to learn that the amateur social work which his assistant was undertaking was actually being inspired by Shelley's example rather than the demands of Christian charity.

Identification with the poet led to triviality; for example, Shelley is soon called in to justify Owen's tendency to doze off when relieved of duty (*CL* p. 109). More importantly, he helped Owen to understand the culture-shock he was going through as he encountered human suffering for the first time, outside the covers of a book. He seems to have been the model for the poems about the poor which Owen began to write at this time. Owen was deeply moved by the burial of a mother and child, and produced a poem on this subject, beginning 'Deep under turfy grass and heavy clay', which is set in the village churchyard. Considering the way in which marriages and funerals are both celebrated inside the church, the poet sounds an unexpected note of anger, rejecting the religiosity expected of the occasion:

> So I rebelled, scorning and mocking such
> As had the ignorant callousness to wed
> On altar steps long frozen by the touch
> Of stretcher after stretcher of our dead . . .

Owen found his sympathies pulling away from the paternalistic do-gooding that he was expected to practise, and in one and the same letter began to challenge literary critical authority and to look at the village ploughmen with new eyes:

'The Revolutionary Ideals, crossing the Channel into England, inspired the British School of revolt and reconstruction in Burns, Shelley, Byron, Wordsworth, Coleridge and Tennyson, *till its fires have died down today.*' Have they! They may have in the bosoms of the muses, but not in my breast. . . . From what I hear straight from the tight-pursed lips of wolfish ploughmen in their cottages, I might say there is material ready for another revolution. Perhaps men will *strike*, not with absence from work; but with arms at work. Am I for or against upheaval? I know not; I am not happy in these thoughts . . . (*CL* p. 131)

So Shelley became for Owen a point of reference and a fulcrum on which he could lean to change his beliefs. When he broke with Dunsden he compared it to an incident in Shelley's life: 'This flight of mine from overbearing elders, if it comes off, will only be my version of running away from College (Shelley, Coleridge)' (*CL* p. 175). The week before he left the rectory he talked darkly of 'powers which would shake the foundations of many a spiritual life' (*CL* p. 179). Shelley had used these to convert people to Atheism but Owen was to hold back.

He must have talked constantly of Shelley in the succeeding period for he received the Oxford edition of Shelley for his twenty-first birthday and read it with a student at Bordeaux. What all this represents is the priority of Romantic idealism over religion in Owen's mind. From this time onwards Shelley was not much mentioned in Owen's letters, not because he had been forgotten but because his message had been internalised. His influence as a kind of spiritual role model must be understood as a constant presence in Owen's poetry.

As well as his progressive ideas, Shelley had his mystical side too. The following lines from *Prometheus Unbound* are relevant to the next poem:

> Ere Babylon was dust,
> The Magus Zoroaster, my dead child,
> Met his own image walking in the garden,
> That apparition, sole of men, he saw.
> For know there are two worlds of life and death:
> One that which thou beholdest; but the other
> Is underneath the grave, where do inhabit
> The shadows of all forms that think and live
> Till death unite them and they part no more . . .
> *Prometheus Unbound*, Act 1, ll. 191 ff.

Shelley's poems contain many strange journeys into caverns under the earth in search of hidden knowledge. Returning to Owen himself, this Shelleyan image of the cavern remained with him almost to the end. On 1 September 1918 he wrote to Sassoon after his return to France: 'Serenity Shelley never dreamed of crowns me. Will it last when I shall have gone into Caverns & Abysmals such as he never reserved for his worst daemons?' (*CL* p. 571). With these thoughts in mind, let us turn to 'Strange Meeting'.

Wheels (1919)

Owen had been asked by Edith and Osbert Sitwell to supply poems for their annual anthology, which was published from 1917 onwards. In 1918 Wilfred had been at great pains to secure a copy and become fully aware of their tastes, though they were quite new to him. Seven poems were included in the 1919 volume, which was not of course published until after Owen's death and was dedicated to his memory. One must appreciate the importance of this Modernist setting in establishing Owen's readership.

Strange Meeting

It seemed that out of battle I escaped
Down some profound dull tunnel, long since scooped
Through granites which Titanic wars had groined.
Yet also there encumbered sleepers groaned,
Too fast in thought or death to be bestirred.
Then, as I probed them, one sprang up, and stared
With piteous recognition in fixed eyes,
Lifting distressful hands as if to bless.
And by his smile, I knew that sullen hall.
With a thousand pains that vision's face was grained;
Yet no blood reached there from the upper ground,
And no guns thumped, or down the flues made moan.
'Strange friend,' I said, 'here is no cause to mourn.'
'None,' said the other, 'Save the undone years,
The hopelessness. Whatever hope is yours,
Was my life also; I went hunting wild
After the wildest beauty in the world,
Which lies not calm in eyes, or braided hair,
But mocks the steady running of the hour,
And if it grieves, grieves richlier than here.
For by my glee might many men have laughed,
And of my weeping something has been left,
Which must die now. I mean the truth untold,
The pity of war, the pity war distilled.
Now men will go content with what we spoiled,
Or discontent, boil bloody, and be spilled.
They will be swift with swiftness of the tigress,

None will break ranks, though nations trek from progress.
Courage was mine, and I had mystery;
Wisdom was mine, and I had mastery;
To miss the march of this retreating world
Into vain citadels that are not walled.
Then, when much blood had clogged their chariot-wheels
I would go up and wash them from sweet wells,
Even with truths that lie too deep for taint.
I would have poured my spirit without stint
But not through wounds; not on the cess of war.
Foreheads of men have bled where no wounds were.
I am the enemy you killed, my friend.
I knew you in this dark; for so you frowned
Yesterday through me as you jabbed and killed.
I parried; but my hands were loath and cold.
Let us sleep now . . .'

COMPOSITION AND TEXT USED HERE The poem was probably begun in
January to March 1918 and finished before June 1918. In one of the
lists of poems for the proposed volume it is subtitled or classified
as 'Foolishness of War'. Drafts of the poem exist, and a number
of alterations are important. For example, the dead German once
said:

> I was a German conscript, and your friend

which becomes more effective as

> I am the enemy you killed, my friend.

The text used here is that of *Poems* (1920), through which Owen
became generally available to young people in the 1920s. Note that
in this edition Sassoon, following his interpretation of the MS, omits
the pair to line 9; in most editions line 10 follows as:

> By his dead smile I knew we stood in Hell.

There are many other minor points of difference between this and
subsequent editions, all of which are well worth looking up and
thinking about.

TITLE This is usually said to have been taken from Shelley's *The
Revolt of Islam*, and the arguments which Welland deployed in making this identification are very strong (pp. 99–100). In this famous
stanza Shelley's narrator, after a deep wound has caused him to lose
consciousness, wakens to find himself confronted by the enemy soldier who had inflicted it:

And one whose spear had pierced me, leaned beside,
With quivering lips and humid eyes; – and all
Seemed like some brothers on a journey wide
Gone forth, whom now strange meeting did befall
In a strange land, round one whom they might call
Their friend, their chief, their father, for assay
Of peril, which had saved them from the thrall
Of death, now suffering. Thus the vast array
Of those fraternal bands were reconciled that day.

The Revolt of Islam, Canto V, xiii

This source may also help us to account for the wounding by bayonet and the sense of reconciliation in the poem, but see below. However, the strangeness of the meeting in Owen's story surely lies in the fact that in the world of the dead the speaker meets a reanimated 'sleeper' and that this unknown person turns out to be a virtual image of himself – 'Whatever hope is yours/ Was my life also'. In Romantic iconography such a figure, for example as described in *Prometheus Unbound*, is known as the *doppelgänger*. From his study of Shelley's life Owen would have known that the poet's own image appeared to him at Casa Magni; it spoke to him, saying, 'How long do you mean to be content?'. Welland was also right to look for the *doppelgänger* in such pictorial sources as Rossetti's 'How They Met Themselves'.

PUBLICATION When the poem was published in *Poems* (1920) it was given pride of place, being positioned first in the selection of poems. (Owen had placed this at about No. 21 in his proposed volume, so that the way in which this – of all his poems – has incremented in value was certainly not expected by the author.)

RELATION TO SIMILAR POEM A variant version of the prophetic lines was first published in *The Athenaeum* on 13 August 1920 with the title 'Fragment'.

Earth's wheels run oiled with blood. Forget we that,
Let us turn back to beauty and to thought.
Better break ranks than trek away from progress.
Let us forgo men's minds that are brute natures,
Let us not sup on blood which some say nurtures,
Be we not swift with swiftness of the tigress.

Beauty is yours, and you have mastery;
Wisdom is mine, and I have mystery;
We two will stay behind and keep our troth.

Miss we the march of this retreating world
Into vain citadels that are not walled.
Let us lie out and hold the open truth.

Then when their blood has clogged the chariot wheels
We will go up and wash them from deep wells,
Even the wells we dug too deep for war.

For now we sink from men as pitchers falling,
But men shall raise us up to be their filling,
The same whose faces bled where no wounds were.

While it includes many of the lines from 'Strange Meeting', it is better to read it as if it were a complete and separate poem. As Hibberd says (p. 75), 'this seems to be the exhortation to keep out of the war which he sent to Sassoon in November [1917]'. It suggests a conspiracy of two persons who will 'break ranks' and therefore be able to refresh humanity when the war is over. It gives a positive vision of the future, and although it shares so many of the words of 'Strange Meeting' the total sense of this poem is entirely different.

NARRATIVE A literal reading of 'Strange Meeting' seems almost impossible because of the sheer weight of symbolism. In some kind of dream-state – 'It seemed' (but this is not possible) – the poet descends into one of the many tunnels under the front line. At the end of this journey he states that he has arrived in Hell. There he encounters a German soldier he has recently killed who, instead of demanding revenge, laments the waste of life and wishes to be reconciled. (The latter stages of this fantasy were shared by many patients at psychiatric hospitals like Craiglockhart.)

The way in which the German speaks is so mysterious that it can only be described as oracular. Yet the message which the German gives may also be rendered quite literally in terms of the war:

1 This war is killing off the most sensitive minds, of whom we are examples. Not only will our work be incomplete but the truth about this war will never be told.
2 What remains will be worse. There will be no progress after the war, only the reverse.
3 It is therefore unlikely that reconciliation will be possible.

The German is found to be a friend and, by his rich use of language, a fellow-poet.

AUDITORY IMAGINATION This poem works upon the ear, and must be read aloud. There has been much discussion of the use of half-rhyme in the poem, and sometimes one feels that the audience are rushed in to applaud its use without perhaps having been aware of the device at first hearing. For evidence of the reaction of the first readers of the poem Welland quotes Middleton Murry's review in *The Athenaeum* on 19 February 1921:

I believe that the reader who comes fresh to this poem does not immediately observe the assonant endings. At first he feels only that the blank verse has a mournful, impressive, even oppressive quality of its own; that the poem has a forged unity, a welded and inexorable massiveness. . . .

   The reader looks again and discovers the technical secret; but if he regards it then as an amazing technical innovation, he is in danger of falsifying his own reaction to the poem.

The essence of Murry's case is that this is the art that conceals art. In the first few lines all the sounds need to be assessed together and not just the rhymes, e.g. 'granites' as well as 'groined' and 'groaned'. It can then be seen that the whole sequence of words 'down some profound dull tunnel' is mimetic of the echoing of noise down and along such a structure and that Owen has achieved a unity of sound and sense in describing such reverberation.

   Welland also attributes to Michael Roberts the theory that the sequence of half-rhymes is often from higher to lower register, e.g. moan/mourn, and that this is deliberately intended to be unsettling, even displeasing to the reader (p. 120). Whether this mirrors a world of disharmony – a further extension of the theory – will be considered when we meet the poem 'Exposure'.

IS THE POEM FINISHED? There is considerable debate about this. The MSS do indicate a sense of hurry and various lines are sometimes supplied by editors. Though it is reasonable to assume that the poem is unfinished in the sense that Owen needed to do more work upon it, it is worth asking some questions in order to clarify what the problem is.

   Would this work be a further extension of the narrative or simply a tidying up of the sense? Would it still be presented as a Romantic fragment? Coleridge's 'Kubla Khan' has always been considered more Romantic because it is a fragment – this is all the subconscious Muse would give before the person from Porlock intervened. Similarly here, there is a sense of finality in the last line – how would it continue, without starting an entirely new subject? The transmission from the oracle underneath the earth is over. The dreamer returns to sleep.

COMPARISON WITH DANTE The main idea of the poem is the encounter in the Underworld. 'Hell' seems rather too threatening a concept, and perhaps a shade inappropriate as Hell is what is actually going on in the trenches above; but Owen would be familiar with this translation of Dante's *Inferno* as it was the title used in Cary's version, which he owned. The typical situation in Dante's poem is imitated here. The hero, who has wandered into Hell, encounters people who seem to be inert or preoccupied, but are galvanised into life by questions or simply by the appearance of the living person – 'one sprang up, and stared'. Recognition follows, and usually a long speech is delivered by the dead person to Dante which leads up to the moment and manner of death; sometimes the dead people prophesy or give a message to the upper world.

Since the acquaintance of most English readers with Dante is rudimentary, I don't think that this comparison spoils the first reading of the poem – which is compelling because we don't know what is going to happen. It does, however, seem to clinch the often disputed point as to whether the narrator is also dead; surely he is alive, and visiting Hell in a dream-vision, as Dante did before him.

OTHER LITERARY ECHOES These abound. Yet the enumeration of them does not in this case seem to destroy the poem but rather to reinforce its effect. It is as if a symphony of English poetry and classical allusion was being played behind Owen's poem as he draws upon all his powers. For example, the opening lines of the poem are reminiscent of Keats and in particular of *Hyperion*, which was concerned with 'titanic wars'. 'Chariot-wheels' on the other hand are more Shelleyan and remind us of his visionary poem 'The Triumph of Life'. The descent into the earth in search of truth is archetypal, and appears in so many books that one cannot begin to list them. Such a descent took one into the classical underworld. Oracles are traditionally situated under the earth or in a cleft in the rocks, for example the Cumaean Sybil, the prophetess at Delphi, or Amphiarus, the warrior who was swallowed up by the earth. One could also speculate whether the opening of *Alice in Wonderland* does not contribute the idea of escaping from the present situation by going down a hole in the ground.

ACTUALITY Normally I would want to argue away from personal experience as a source in these poems. Real experiences may inspire a poem, but the poet works on them with a different part of the mind from that which simply relates anecdotes. But with this poem one wants to scream out that it is not simply a rehash of innumerable items from Owen's reading; poets are not always dependent on literary sources. In his own battle experience Owen had fallen down 'into a kind of well' (13/14 March 1917) and lost consciousness; in mid-April of the same year (in a passage already quoted but this time note my italics) Owen describes how:

> *Before I awoke*, I was blown in the air [by a shell] . . . I passed most of the following days *in a railway cutting, in a hole* just big enough to

lie in, and *covered* with corrugated iron. My *brother* officer of B Coy,
2/Lt Gaukroger *lay opposite in a similar hole*. But he was covered
with earth, and no relief will ever relieve him . . . (*CL* p. 452)

This experience affected him deeply and may have triggered his
shell-shock. Owen knew about hand-to-hand fighting and must have
felt remorse about the casualties he had caused. And Craiglockhart
Hospital was full of encumbered sleepers who groaned.

CONCLUSION The poem is truly oracular. When it was published it
sounded like a voice from beyond the grave; it fitted the mood of the
1920s. Sassoon called the poem Owen's 'passport to immortality,
and his elegy to the unknown warriors of all nations'. At a later
stage, like Yeats's exactly contemporary poem 'The Second Coming', the prophecy of the trek from progress must have seemed to be
a warning of the coming of fascism to Europe.

New Inspirations: Sassoon

After leaving him, I wrote something in Sassoon's style, which I
may as well send you, since you ask for the latest. (*CL* p. 485)

On 22 August 1917, shortly after meeting Siegfried Sassoon, Wilfred
Owen wrote the above note, which refers to his latest poem 'The
Dead-Beat'. One needs to consider how shocked the recipient, Leslie
Gunston, would have been with this conversational and slangy offer-
ing, but Owen forces it upon him. In the same week Owen sent
Sassoon's volume – *The Old Huntsman and Other Poems* – to his father
with a request for his critical opinions. By these means he was, no
doubt, getting rid of a lot of irritation with those who could not keep
pace with him.

Sassoon's place in the history of Great War poetry has already
been indicated; writing after the Somme battle, he introduced the
third stage of war poetry, bringing to bear on the situation both a
new perception of events and a new style of expression. Sassoon
broke the rules of self-censorship which had governed British discourse about the war for all ranks. The first rule was basic to the
British character: you might be having a terrible time at the front
but you sent cheerful letters home all the same. In mentioning the
arrival of the new poet at Craiglockhart, but before meeting him,
Wilfred explains to his mother about Sassoon's famous letter and
adds that he was 'too plain-spoken' (*CL* p. 485).

Keeping the reality of war from the civilians meant, however, that
they did not hear about the sufferings of the troops. Therefore the
troops were not perceived to be suffering. And so the second rule
applied: that anybody who did refer to these matters must have gone

'soft'. But 'Mad Jack', as Sassoon was called, with his Military Cross for daring, could not be described as 'soft'. Therefore he must have really gone mad.

As has already been suggested, the real difficulty lay with the capabilities of the English language itself in its current state rather than with individuals. The kit of words with which poets approached the experience of war was inadequate. (More literally, the volumes of poetry which some poets took with them into battle had other uses than those expected; Blunden's copy of Hardy, kept in his breast-pocket throughout the conflict, at least served as body-armour when all else failed.) Even the most modern English poets – the Georgians – had nothing to say about war at all. After the Somme too much had become bottled up in the collective psyche and demanded to break out into expression. In his poems Sassoon wanted to speak for all the soldiers, not just for himself. So it is not surprising that Owen, writing to his mother again after a short interval, gives another warning about the kind of discourse she is to expect:

> You may be a little shocked by Sassoon's language. He is of course, with W.E.O. practically the only one in the place who doesn't swear conversationally. He is simply honest about the war. (*CL* p. 493)

In his volume *The Old Huntsman and Other Poems*, the route by which Sassoon had reached this point is traced out from the first stages of the war. Besides the more conventional early poems, the volume contains satires and short narratives about life in the trenches. It was these that most excited Owen:

> Nothing like his trench life sketches has ever been written or ever will be written. Shakespeare reads vapid after these. Not of course because Sassoon is a greater artist, but because of the subjects, I mean. (*CL* p. 484)

It seems never to have occurred to Owen to write in this way himself about the war before, which strikes us as most strange. He had continued to exchange beautiful poems with Leslie throughout that summer, which is why 'The Dead-Beat' would have shocked his friend. Sassoon had not only taught Owen that poetry could be written about their past experience of war; then and there in the hospital he was producing work which was an immediate response to the present situation:

> Do they matter? – those dreams from the pit? . . .
> You can drink and forget and be glad,
> And people won't say that you're mad;
> For they'll know that you've fought for your country
> And no one will worry a bit.
>
> 'Does it matter?', last stanza

Given this example, Owen swung into action and produced nearly all the poetry that we remember him by in the space of twelve months.

The Sentry

We'd found an old Boche dug-out, and he knew,
And gave us hell, for shell on frantic shell
Hammered on top, but never quite burst through.
Rain, guttering down in waterfalls of slime
Kept slush waist high that, rising hour by hour,
Choked up the steps too thick with clay to climb.
What murk of air remained stank old, and sour
With fumes of whizz-bangs, and the smell of men
Who'd lived there years, and left their curse in the den,
If not their corpses . . .
                            There we herded from the blast
Of whizz-bangs, but one found our door at last.
Buffeting eyes and breath, snuffing the candles.
And thud! flump! thud! down the steep steps came thumping
And splashing in the flood, deluging muck –
The sentry's body; then, his rifle, handles
Of old Boche bombs, and mud in ruck and ruck.
We dredged him up, for killed, until he whined
'O sir, my eyes – I'm blind – I'm blind, I'm blind!'
Coaxing, I held a flame against his lids
And said if he could see the least blurred light
He was not blind; in time he'd get all right.
'I can't,' he sobbed. Eyeballs, huge-bulged like squids
Watch my dreams still; but I forgot him there
In posting next for duty, and sending a scout
To beg a stretcher somewhere, and floundering about
To other posts under the shrieking air.
Those other wretches, how they bled and spewed,
And one who would have drowned himself for good, –
I try not to remember these things now.
Let dread hark back for one word only: how
Half-listening to that sentry's moans and jumps,
And the wild chattering of his broken teeth,
Renewed most horribly whenever crumps
Pummelled the roof and slogged the air beneath –
Through the dense din, I say, we heard him shout
'I see your lights!' But ours had long died out.

PUBLICATION *Wheels* (1919). 'I have done something towards my Contribution to *Wheels*' (*CL* p. 569) implies that Owen did send the

Sitwells several poems, including presumably the poem printed here. Because of his death the poems did not appear until a year later, and by then others would have had a hand in the selection. Once again the text printed here is that of *Poems* (1920).

COMPOSITION There are various drafts of the poem with minor variations only, apart from line 17 where Stallworthy reads 'We dredged it up – for dead'. Stallworthy says that this poem was probably begun in late 1917 but not finished until September 1918.[2] It may have been put to one side for some time, though it is possible that this poem features in one of Owen's lists as 'The Light', classified as 'Description'; it was also called 'The Blind' on 22 September 1918.

ACTUALITY Owen went through an experience similar to that in the poem and described it immediately afterwards in a letter of 16 January 1917. Since he asks at the end that portions should be typed he would probably have been able to have access to a copy while preparing the poem should he have needed to. A number of verbal resemblances in what follows – apart from the main incident – seem to indicate that the letter was re-used to write the poem. It is interesting to note that Keats seems to have referred to his letters in the same way.

> Three quarters dead, I mean each of us ¾ dead, we reached the dug-out, and relieved the wretches therein . . .
>
> My dug-out held 25 men tight packed. Water filled it to a depth of 1 or 2 feet, leaving say 4 feet of air.
>
> One entrance had been blown in & blocked.
>
> So far, the other remained.
>
> The Germans knew we were staying there and decided we shouldn't.
>
> Those fifty hours were the agony of my happy life . . .
>
> I nearly broke down and let myself drown in the water that was now slowly rising over my knees.
>
> Towards 6 o'clock, when, I suppose, you would be going to church, the shelling grew less intense and less accurate: so that I was mercifully helped to do my duty and crawl, wade, climb and flounder over No Man's Land to visit my other post. It took me half an hour to move about 150 yards. . . .
>
> In the Platoon on my left the sentries over the dug-out were blown to nothing. One of these poor fellows was my first servant whom I rejected. If I had kept him he would have lived, for servants don't do Sentry Duty. I kept my own sentries half way down the stairs during the more terrific bombardment. In spite of this one lad was blown down and, I am afraid, blinded. (*CL* pp. 427–8)

In spite of all this, it does not follow that Owen is to be *identified* with the officer in the poem, which is a fiction created to make a point.

THE STORY AND ITS TELLING This is presented as a war story, which begins with the storyteller taking us into his confidence. This is an old hand's tone of voice, with occasional bad jokes. 'Curse' and 'corpses' pun, and words like 'whizz-bang' are specialised vocabulary. Rapidly the past is recreated so skilfully – with sounds and smells and tactile sensations – that at first it feels like the present; and so it unrolls as a realistic description, a 'scene', a vignette. And this realism does dominate most of the poem so that it could simply be filed under 'Description' as in the poem-lists. But is this enough? Even as a simple story it must be classified as a 'wonder-tale', because of the appalling things that happen, and secondly as a kind of 'joke with a punch-line' because of the sentry's mistake at the end.

There are several points of comparison to other better-known poems which lead us to see that more is going on under the surface. First there is the striving to escape from the battle to the comparative safety of underground, as in 'Strange Meeting'. Then there is the close resemblance of the victim of the incident to the gassed man in 'Dulce et Decorum Est'. As in that poem the dreams of the present (i.e. Craiglockhart Hospital or later) are brought in; the eyes of the suffering man are particularly frightening, too. In this poem the 'eye-balls, huge-bulged like squids', watch my dreams still'.

And so it turns into a hospital story – this is an example of a 'dream from the pit'. The sentry is closely observed as he deteriorates. He is either going through the stages of shock, or having a more serious breakdown, i.e. he provides an illustration of a classic case of shell-shock since he has been 'blown down'. The officer, too, who tells the story, is open to criticism; he flounders about, and seems to have mislaid his responsibilities.

POINT OF VIEW This poem is similar to one by Blunden ('Pillbox') and one by Sassoon ('Died of wounds'). I am not suggesting that these could be sources, only that the experience was not uncommon. The reason it resembles both of these is because it shows the officer's view of the sufferings of the troops. In the poem the narrator often uses 'we' and 'us' but this in fact disguises the truth. It is not a collective leadership. The blind man calls on his officer to save him. In the third section of the poem the chaos spreads even further; remember that in the letter it was Owen who wanted to drown himself. Although in real terms the narrator is not responsible for the fortunes of war, he is haunted by the incident. He feels he is responsible for what has happened to his men.

THE GREATER SYMBOLISM If – and there are a lot of imponderables here – this is read as a very late poem by Owen in which he looks back on this scene as a incident *representative* of the whole of the Great War, then it might be possible to go along with those readers who see the whole poem as severely judgemental. For Silkin, in his edition, the light that goes out is 'the symbolic representation, or rather, symbolic counterpart, of the extinction of life, hope, energy, creation, value, in our souls . . . such is the destructive power of war' (Silkin p. 93). Douglas Kerr sees the total eclipse of all the lights of society – the stress is on the word 'our' as much as on the 'lights':

> For Owen, at the story's end, all 'our' leading lights have failed – officers, ruling class, institutions, traditions, the enlightenment of science, and the kindly light of religion – all authorities and beliefs, all ranks and all distinctions are blotted out in the dark, where the blind lead the blind. (Kerr p. 228)

Faced with this reading, the end of the poem begins to aspire to greatness; it might be compared to such classic high points as the ending of *The Dunciad* by Alexander Pope:

> Nor public flame, nor private, dares to shine;
> Nor human spark is left, nor glimpse divine!
> Lo! thy dread empire, Chaos! is restor'd;
> Light dies before thy uncreating word;
> Thy hand, great Anarch! lets the curtain fall,
> And universal darkness buries all.

And certainly in the poetic context in which Owen flourished, bridging as it does the nineteenth and twentieth centuries, comparison with the central themes of Arnold's 'Dover Beach', Browning's 'Childe Roland' or Eliot's *The Waste Land* do not seem out of order. Here is another night-battle, here another medieval knight who failed to ask the right questions; here indeed Childe Roland to the Dark Tower came.

Poems (1920)

In 1920 Sassoon was able to publish a generous selection of Owen's poems which was an approximation in size and content to the volume which Owen had planned in his lists of 1918. (There was no intention, as in recent editions, to track down and preserve all that Owen had written.) This volume was honed down so that it only contained the best of the war poems. 'Miners', for example, which Owen had intended to go first, was left out and was replaced by 'Strange Meeting'. The collection would have interested both traditionalists and 'Modernists', though remember that we are talking of

1920, a time untouched by such Modernist classics as *The Waste Land*. Traditionalists might well have been impressed by certain poems of the Ode type, e.g. 'Greater Love', which, as has often been commented, bears an ironic relationship to Swinburne. One wonders how far the irony was noticed, for these verses were singled out for educational use and appeared in Methuen's 1922 anthology for schools. From the many great and canonical works by Owen which appeared for the first time in the 1920 volume, let us look at 'Exposure' as an example of a poem with the opposite appeal: stylistically this could only be read as an attack on the kind of poetry inherited from the nineteenth century, and therefore in some sense 'modern'.

Exposure

I

Our brains ache, in the merciless iced east winds that knife us . . .
Wearied we keep awake because the night is silent . . .
Low, drooping flares confuse our memory of the salient . . .
Worried by silence, sentries whisper, curious, nervous,
   But nothing happens.

Watching, we hear the mad gusts tugging on the wire,
Like twitching agonies of men among its brambles.
Northward incessantly, the flickering gunnery rumbles,
Far off, like a dull rumour of some other war.
   What are we doing here?

The poignant misery of dawn begins to grow . . .
We only know war lasts, rain soaks, and clouds sag stormy.
Dawn massing in the east her melancholy army
Attacks once more in ranks on shivering ranks of gray,
   But nothing happens.

Sudden successive flights of bullets streak the silence.
Less deadly than the air that shudders black with snow
With sidelong flowing flakes that flock, pause, and renew
We watch them wandering up and down the wind's nonchalance,
   But nothing happens.

II

Pale flakes with fingering stealth come feeling for our faces –
We cringe in holes, back on forgotten dreams, and stare,
 snow-dazed
Deep into grassier ditches. So we drowse, sun-dozed,
Littered with blossoms trickling where the blackbird fusses.
   Is it that we are dying?

Slowly our ghosts drag home: glimpsing the sunk fires glozed
With crusted dark-red jewels; crickets jingle there;

For hours the innocent mice rejoice: the house is theirs;
Shutters and doors all closed: on us the doors are closed –
    We turn back to our dying.

Since we believe not otherwise can kind fires burn;
Nor ever suns smile true on child, or field, or fruit.
For God's invincible spring our love is made afraid;
Therefore, not loath, we lie out here; therefore were born,
    For love of God seems dying.

To-night, His frost will fasten on this mud and us,
Shrivelling many hands and puckering foreheads crisp.
The burying-party, picks and shovels in their shaking grasp,
Pause over half-known faces. All their eyes are ice,
    But nothing happens.

COMPOSITION The composition of this poem seems to have been
spread over a long period. In the bottom corner of the main MS is
the date 'Feb 1916', presumably referring not to the date of the text
in its final state but to the original draft; however, on stylistic grounds
among others, this is normally considered to be an error. The poem
is usually thought to have been composed in approximately December 1917. An item called 'Nothing happens' is featured in both the
lists for a proposed volume which Owen drew up in May/June
1918. On the other hand what appear to be early drafts for the first
two stanzas are on paper which is associated with September 1918,
when Owen was at Amiens waiting to go up to the front line. The
dating of this poem is therefore a major problem which I propose to
debate later in this commentary.

PUBLICATION In *Poems* (1920). This is the text used above. Sassoon
divided the poem into two halves, and has a number of readings, e.g.
'knife' for 'knive' in the first stanza, which do not figure in the
commonly received version. There are serious problems of meaning
associated with the variant readings of this poem, particularly in the
last stanza. Here Jon Stallworthy – rightly in my opinion – reads
'this' for 'His' in the first line. He retains 'ice' instead of what looks
like 'red' in the MS for the ending of the fourth line.

TITLE The title could mean exposure to enemy attack or *to cold*. In
fact it is a description of an extreme experience of cold weather,
and the fact that they are in the front line seems to be of less
importance.

NARRATIVE The soldiers are presumably in a salient, which, being
a bulge into enemy territory, would mean that they were exposed

to enemy fire from three sides, and they are extremely tense and 'nervous'. Alternatively it is a German salient which is being attacked by them. It is winter, it is dark, the snow falls. But in fact everything is quiet. Apart from the single flight of bullets in stanza 4 their main enemy is in fact nature. The dawn begins to appear. The cold is so intense that one can only hazard that they begin to hallucinate, dreaming of a home which is warm but excludes them. They attempt to come to a metaphysical explanation of why they are out there, and affirm their commitment to the war, but God's wishes are not easy to establish. In the last stanza a burying party is observed, and the return of night with its intense cold is anticipated.

DATE (1) In February 1916 Owen was undergoing his first experiences of guard duty (e.g. *CL* p. 367; *CL* p. 382), always traumatic for a soldier and a clear break with the rhythm of civilian life, where one does not normally stay out all night. Winters can be cold in England as well as elsewhere – see the letters of 19 Nov 1915 where he reports 'rifles frozen over with snow' (*CL* p. 366) and 1 Feb 1916 'all night I was persuaded I should not warm my limbs again in this world' (*CL* p. 378). One might speculate that the poem could have been in its first form a description of the long night on guard and the rumble could refer to the anti-aircraft guns outside East London. (Most of the poem is curiously quiet for the front line, but Owen was in an area affected by Zeppelin raids in February 1916 (*CL* p. 377)). The poet's thoughts go round in circles, coming back to the refrain 'But nothing happens'. It is this line which could fit the lack of events on guard duty or, in early 1916, could be an echo of the famous phrase 'all quiet on the Western front'. The soldiers' sentiments about home, although they seem to get muddled, are based ultimately upon such lyrics as 'Keep the home fires burning'; they fit the period 1915/16, and the kind of discussions which soldiers would have had about their motivation for fighting *before* such events as the Battle of the Somme.

While all this is pure speculation, it is possible to check the theory – or some of it – by looking at the core of the poem: stanzas 3–7, less the bullets, which take up one line. Portions of the other stanzas could also fit this account, but are not needed.

DATE (2) Blunden thought the poem was a description of an actual experience in the front line and that it referred to Owen's period of service in February 1917; he thought that the MS note was a slip and that Owen had misdated these events by a year. In support of this theory we may note that Owen described an actual experience which appears to fit the events in the poem in a letter of 4 February 1917:

in this place my Platoon had no Dug-Outs, but had to lie in the
snow under the deadly wind . . .

The marvel is that we did not all die of cold. As a matter of fact
only one of my party actually froze to death before he could be
got back, but I am not able to tell how many have ended in
hospital. I had no real casualties from shelling . . .

My feet ached until they could ache no more, and so they
temporarily died. I was kept warm by the ardour of Life within
me. I forgot hunger in the hunger for life. The intensity of your
Love reached me and kept me living. I thought of you and Mary
without a break all the time. I cannot say I felt any fear. . . . (*CL*
p. 430)

This letter is a very convincing source. More importantly, in terms of
establishing the date, Siegfried Sassoon was convinced that 'Exposure' had been written before he met Owen and felt that February
1917 was about right. Several authorities, e.g. Jon Silkin, argue in
favour of this date as the point where the poem began to form in
Owen's mind.

DATE (3) Owen quotes the refrain 'Nothing Happens' in a letter to
his mother on 22 April 1918, implying that the poem is in existence by then. Thereafter we have dates mentioned above under
'Composition'.

All in all it would seem that the protracted gestation of the poem
and its very late revision, when Owen was less sure of his religious
attitudes, may account for some of the problems with the 'message'
of this text.

THE THOUGHT OF THE POEM Owen classified 'Nothing happens' as
'Description' in one of his lists of poems for publication; to us this
would seem a little understated. The original title, and the use of the
same words in the refrain, would emphasise the tension of the ex-
pectant soldiers in stanza 1 in contrast to the intense boredom of the
actual duties they are called on to perform. Possibly as a result of
inexperience, they are waiting for some kind of action to develop,
but all that is required is that they endure. When the refrain is
discarded for phrases like 'What are we doing here?' and 'Is it that
we are dying?', the stuffing seems to have fallen out of their heroism.
Stanzas 5, 6 and 7 are difficult to put together at first; they progress
from (5) the illusion that it is a sun-lit spring day to (6) a rather self-
pitying state; they are in the period immediately after death and
their ghosts return to their homes in the middle of the night. Though
they glimpse the 'home fires', they have died down (or been banked
up?). Though the animal kingdom has taken over the house (in their

place?), the ghosts are forbidden to enter. Therefore (7), and the main argument seems to be placed here, the soldiers must continue their travail because it will ensure the future, when the fires will burn *up*, the sun *truly* shine, and 'God's invincible spring' *will* come.

This summary does not do justice to a number of major difficulties in these three stanzas. What is the force of 'innocent' in the 'innocent mice'? Why are the ghosts unable to enter their homes? Are they barred out by unsympathetic civilians who have forgotten them? Or have they simply arrived when everybody has gone to bed? Or is it dream-logic, which tells them that the house is deserted because they have deserted the front line? Finally, what has happened to the 'love of God'? Is His Love dying? Or, taking the words the other way, is our love for Him declining? The religious emphasis on 'His frost' in the last stanza – though note the amended text by Stallworthy which gets rid of this – would seem to show a punitive sky- or weather-God; if it is the correct reading it is particularly difficult and not clearly integrated into the poem.

THE LANGUAGE At first all the force of this poem is aimed at dislodging romantic ideas of battle with an extreme use of the rhetoric of Romantic poetry. Line 1 is parodic of the 'Ode to a Nightingale', which begins 'My heart aches' and then takes the long 'a' sound on into rhymes on 'pains' and 'drains'. 'Our brains ache in the iced east winds' is full of Keatsian attention to the detail of language almost to a fault, and 'knife/knive' continues the vowel-sound of 'ice' through to the end of the line. Such a line is also difficult if not painful to read aloud, miming the experience of the wind-chill it describes.

In the early stanzas the effects of bleakness are very tough indeed. Here the discordant jarring of the pararhyme is indeed 'nervous' if not odd. The unrhymed refrain is clipped back from the normal length of line as if the soldiers' statements are bitten off in the cold wind. Also one senses that the soldiers seem to have undergone a middle-class 'character-training' – to say nothing or to keep it short.

All this loosens up in the central stanzas, which keep to the Keatsian theme, this time exploring 'drowsy numbness'. Here again this is a parody of a kind of Romantic reverie, e.g. Coleridge's 'Frost at Midnight'. Of course as the soldiers are on official military duty they can't fall asleep; they remain on the verge of losing consciousness.

The images of home are detailed like charms against the cold, and the associations of ideas have a literary origin. Of course a warm fire is needed here, though 'glozed' is worrying as it ought to mean 'deceitful'; and the hearth brings in the 'cricket'. What are the mice doing, except miming the 'innocent' actions of children's stories? As an image of security and warmth 'the brown mice bob' in Yeats's poem 'The Stolen Child'.

PARARHYME: ITS SUCCESS AND ORIGIN The amazing technical skill that
Owen developed is shown in the assonance and half-rhyme in this
poem; notice how the device works against closure, leaving the reader
on edge. This leads in each stanza to the final unrhymed half-line,
which ought not to close either, but in fact brings its own kind of
relief, as from a gnawing pain.

Denis Welland reminds us how much Owen admired Swinburne
and suggests that the device of pararhyme was an antidote to
Swinburne's mechanical chiming. Indeed a volume of Swinburne
was in Owen's pocket at the last, and all this leads one to consider
whether there is a Swinburne poem which is somehow acting as the
subtext to 'Exposure'. Certainly 'A Forsaken Garden' with the short
'refrain' at the end of its stanzas, 'Love lies dead', has a similar kind
of patterning and melancholy sentiment.

The origin of half-rhyme in Owen's thinking has sometimes been
traced to a curious phrase in a letter of 10 April 1916: 'We had
Night Operations again. I was isolated scouting – felt like scooting'
(*CL* p. 390). This once again brings us back to early 1916 in attempt-
ing to place the origins of this poem, and may indicate that pararhyme
was always part of it.

The gates of Modernism

It is now time to assess the final stages of Owen's work and the
position of his poetic theory and practice (in 1917 and 1918) with
reference to his contemporaries. To recapitulate, it is true that he
may have begun to write with considerable disadvantages in education and awareness, compared to say Sassoon and Robert Graves.
On the other hand, it is important to see that Owen, like any other
poet maturing in the period 1910–17, is stuck between the last phase
of Wildean aestheticism – which had now come to power as a highly
influential poetic force in 'literary circles' – and the new Georgians.
Though these plain-spoken decent chaps were supposed to have
made their impress with the new reign and the first *Georgian Poetry*
anthology in 1912, they still hadn't taken over the literary establishment yet, but were always about to; hence Owen's initial pleasure in
being hailed as a Georgian. He wrote in a letter to his mother on the
last day of 1917:

> I go out of this year a Poet, my dear Mother, as which I did not
> enter it. I am held peer by the Georgians; I am a poet's poet. (*CL*
> p. 521)

In case we feel that Owen is backing the wrong party in terms of the
future, it is important also to see that Ezra Pound and T.S. Eliot,

though actually writing and beginning to publish at this time, were simply *unknown* to Owen and the majority of people in 1917.

Owen's poet-friends were not so enamoured of the Georgians. Robert Graves eventually dismissed them as 'principally concerned with Nature and love and leisure and old age and childhood and animals and sleep and similar uncontroversial subjects'; they knew nothing of the 'grinding hardship of trench-service'. Owen seems to have worked this out for himself, and began to push forward into new territory ahead of Graves and Sassoon. Already by May 1918, his poems were beginning to show a new crispness in their diction and an awareness of industrial imagery; for example, 'The Send-Off' has 'darkening lanes' and 'a casual tramp' like a Georgian poem, but 'the siding-shed' and the mechanised brutality of

> . . . unmoved, signals nodded, and a lamp
> Winked to the guard

shows that the soldiers are simply part of an inhuman process. By mid-1918 Owen had met the representatives of another school of modern poetry – the Sitwells. In July he writes to Osbert:

> Last week I broke out of camp to order *Wheels*, 1917. Canning [the Scarborough bookshop] refused to stock copies. I persisted so long that the Young Lady loudly declared she knew all along that I was 'Osbert himself'. This caused a consternation throughout the crowded shop; but I got the last laugh by – 'No, Madam; the book is by a friend of mine, Miss Sitwell'. (*CL* p. 562)

His new style, with its unexpected (and almost foreign?) feelings for other people and more urban imagery, is illustrated in the next poems. But they were never finished, and were therefore omitted from Sassoon's volume in 1920.

The Poems of Wilfred Owen (1931)

When an enlarged collection of the poems was assembled by Edmund Blunden, the text had the benefit of a careful and sympathetic editor. The received canon was now extended and Blunden tried to make sense of all the manuscripts which he was able to call on at that time. When studying these new poems in his versions, it is important to understand that subsequent editions print some of them with revised and improved readings; but the later editors have simply presented alternative versions of these fragmentary texts and it does not follow that Blunden's judgements are necessarily invalidated by the passage of time.

The roads also

The roads also have their wistful rest,
When the weathercocks perch still and roost,
And the town is [quiet like] a candle-lit room –
The streets also dream their dream.

The old houses muse of the old days
And their fond trees leaning on them doze,
On their steps chatter and clatter stops,
On their doors a strange hand taps.

Men remember alien [   ] ardours
As the dusk unearths old mournful odours.
In the garden unborn child souls wail
And the dead scribble on walls.

Though their own child cry for them in tears,
Women weep but hear no sound upstairs.
They believe in loves they had not lived
And in passion past the reach of the stairs
    To the world's towers or stars.

COMPOSITION Spring or summer of 1918. Hibberd is probably right
to think that this draws on the kind of imagery used in the *Wheels*
anthology, so making this a poem of July or later. Two different
manuscripts of the poem have survived. The other one reads:

The roads also have their wistful rest
When the weather cocks perch still and roost
[And the looks of men turn kind to clocks
And the trams go empty to their drome.
    The streets also dream their dream.]

The old houses muse of the old days,
And their fond trees lean on them and doze.
On their steps chatter and clatter stops,
For the cries of other times hold men
    And they [hear] the [unknown] moan.

They remember alien ardours and far futures,
And the smiles not seen in happy features.
Their begetters call them from the gutters.
In the garden unborn child souls wail
    And the dead scribble on walls.

Stallworthy combines these three stanzas with the last one of the first
version to make a matching five-line stanza throughout the text.

COMMENT The images seem quite amazing for Owen, from the drome for the trams to the strange lines about the child-souls and the dead in stanza 3. It matches various paintings of this period which Owen never mentions (but could just have seen?) with their machine-age references and angular aesthetics – I am thinking of Christopher Nevinson and William Roberts. Does this represent some late harvest of his years in France? Kerr (pp. 259–64) invokes Baudelaire as the source of Owen's modernism in this and other poems.

CONCLUSION Though the emotion in the poem seems to be observed from outside and handled in a rather distant way compared to earlier Owen, it is surely a compassionate poem about a deserted town and the civilian population's attempt to comprehend the war. It is therefore a development of his war poetry, and perhaps a rejection of Sassoon's view that the civilians were largely untouched by the conflict. However, you could say against this that the war is never mentioned. This exercise in a new mode is a striking anticipation of the poetry of W.H. Auden, with the unexplained weeping and the indifference of the coolly presented Midland townscape.

It is worth comparing another poem of roughly the same date, 'The Calls', which also exists in two versions; the poet lists the various noises and events of the day, feigns indolence and appears to spurn them; at the end he decides to listen to 'the sighs of men, that have no skill/To speak of their distress' and to 'go' (back into the front line?). The poem is usually taken to record his decision to return willingly to France. In another poem of this period, 'The Kind Ghosts', an air of mystery prevails. If obscurity is one of the marks of Modernism this poem could represent a movement towards the work of Eliot and others in the 1920s.

The Kind Ghosts

She sleeps on soft, last breaths; but no ghost looms
Out of the stillness of her palace wall,
Her wall of boys on boys and dooms on dooms.

She dreams of golden gardens and sweet glooms,
Not marvelling why her roses never fall
Nor what red mouths were torn to make their blooms.

The shades keep down which well might roam her hall.
Quiet their blood lies in her crimson rooms
And she is not afraid of their footfall.

They move not from her tapestries, their pall,
Nor pace her terraces, their hecatombs,
Lest aught she be disturbed or grieved at all.

COMPOSITION The only surviving manuscript is dated 30 July 1918.

PUBLICATION In Blunden's edition as above.

FORM The poem is an incomplete villanelle, again showing the influence of French literature. Half-rhyme is therefore not part of the required scheme and Owen keeps to a limited choice of full rhymes.

INTERPRETATIONS It is not clear what 'she' represents, and various offerings have included a mother-figure (possibly reflecting some irritation with the somnolence of Owen's own mother), or, more generally, the female representation of civilian patriotism, a kind of Britannia. The quietness of the poem does not allow us at first to grasp the horror. Her palace wall is made up of corpses, both a horrific dream-vision and perhaps a literal recollection of the masses of unburied dead along the front line. The point of the poem seems to be that she does not know this, and that the ghosts of the dead are too gentlemanly to enlighten her ignorance. Why, if they are the war-dead, these ghosts are 'kind' remains obscure – certainly they would not have been so quiet in the days when Owen was most influenced by Sassoon.

DIFFICULTIES Since, if we follow this interpretation, the whole poem must be ironic, it is amazing what care has gone into it. In the manuscript all the alliterations and other kinds of verbal artistry are carefully marked out. 'Hecatomb' means an enormous sacrifice to the gods, literally a hundred oxen; these massive killings sometimes took place on long stone structures, and this would fit the sense here. There are hints of sexual violence in the poem, with the torn 'red mouths' of line 6. Once again, Swinburne, Wilde and the decadents lurk in the background; one thinks of Wilde's made-up fairytales, and of figures like Salome. Perhaps this is a 'perverse' imitation of the story of the Sleeping Beauty.

CONCLUSION The poem is certainly odd, and its intentions are not clear at all; perhaps it seems to be more nasty and vicious in its implications than it really was meant to be. I suppose it could be an attempt to imagine a goddess of the dead, who garners in the slain like some kind of gentle Valkyrie, and therefore earns their respect. My own theory is that this poem is not about the war at all, but is the beginning of an attempt to retell the story of the Gorgon, Medusa; there was a version of the legend in which she was represented as a beautiful woman. Perseus killed her while she slept. A poem on Perseus is listed in the projects for May 1918 (see p. 92).

Religion and humanity

Blunden also turned up one or two war poems that had been missed by Sassoon, and it seems appropriate to end with a more typical work by Owen that reflects upon the religious implications of the war, demonstrating once again the very seared conscience.

At a Calvary near the Ancre

One ever hangs where shelled roads part.
In this war He too lost a limb,
But His disciples hide apart;
And now the Soldiers bear with Him.

Near Golgotha strolls many a priest,
And in their faces there is pride
That they were flesh-marked by the Beast
By whom the gentle Christ's denied.

The scribes on all the people shove
And bawl allegiance to the state,
But they who love the greater love
Lay down their life; they do not hate.

COMPOSITION This is usually placed at about August–October 1917 but there is no evidence. The only manuscript is in fact an undated transcript by Susan Owen. The poem is probably connected with 'Le Christianisme' which seems to be slightly later than the date suggested above. Another possible clue is the epigram about the crucifixion which Osbert Sitwell sent to Owen in July 1918, which concludes:

. . . then Jesus died –
But Monsieur Clemenceau is fully satisfied! (quoted in *CL* p. 561)

Owen greatly admired this poem and may have wanted to imitate it.

PUBLICATION Blunden's edition as discussed above.

COMMENT The poem begins as a kind of epigram and the expression is crystal clear. The main idea is that beside the road there is a wayside shrine: the Calvary, representing the Crucifixion. As Evangelically trained Protestants, Owen and most of his fellow-soldiers would not have been able to take this seriously. The conversational aside – 'In this war He too lost a limb' – is almost too casual. But here, one feels, Owen's long residence in France has enabled him to deal with this. He is able to project himself into sympathy with the broken figure and to see how the image of Christ, and therefore by easy transfer Christ Himself, shares the soldiers' pains and has, literally, suffered amputation. This serves to liken Christ to any other wounded soldier, and so he is accepted by the troops as a fellow-sufferer. As in the Bible account of Christ's passion, the disciples are nowhere to be seen; Christ is once again in the company of soldiers as He was then. Notice how the giving of a capital letter – 'Soldiers' – gives them their special, almost sanctified place as companions of Christ in extremity as they were in the Gospel account; 'priest' and 'scribes' do not however receive this honour. This time the soldiers do not mock him but 'bear with Him', both meanings are possible. They tolerate and they suffer with him.

The poem then becomes fiercely anti-clerical. Golgotha is 'the place of the skull' and so immediately identified with a Great War battlefield. The priests are proud that they have been slightly wounded in the flesh by Germany, which is, in their blustering propaganda, 'The Beast who denies Christ'. But the poem is clever and will not allow such a simple reading. If Christ is gentle, what are these priests – who are meant to be unwarlike – showing by their swaggering ('strolls')? Surely that they are 'flesh-marked' by the Devil:

> If any man worship the beast and his image and receive his mark in his forehead, or in his hand (Revelation 14:9)

and are therefore worshippers of the anti-Christian values of war.

Meanwhile, in the third stanza, the word 'scribes' carries both the biblical meaning of learned men or teachers, and the modern meaning of journalists (like Bottomley) who harangue the people in the name of patriotism. But the soldiers are compelled to lay down their lives and they do this without showing the fierce hatred generated by the two kinds of propagandist; the structure of three kinds of observers may also owe something to the story of the Good Samaritan.

RESONANCES Such an account of the poem – as epigram – cannot do justice to its nobility and the way in which it stimulates deeper emotions; these in turn call up further echoes in religion and literature. The Christ who 'ever' (casual use) hangs beside the soldiers on the battlefield is there for 'ever' (religious use), and what this means can only, I suppose, be expressed in such biblical quotations as:

> Is it nothing to you, all ye that pass by? behold and see if there be any sorrow like unto my sorrow . . . (Lamentations of Jeremiah 1:12)

and this is what the soldiers 'bear with Him'. One thinks of pictures by David Jones which illustrate the religious truths experienced by the soldiers in the Great War.

'The parting of the ways' in 'shelled roads part' carries similar double meanings, one of the ways presumably leading to the front line and therefore to death; it is appropriate for the image of Christ to be displayed at this juncture. Two kinds of conduct are outlined in the poem, and it is the soldiers who imitate Christ and will proceed to reconciliation because 'they do not hate'. The much misused phrase about 'greater love' is finally seen to encompass something more than the mere state-serving patriotism which it had been twisted to mean.

CONCLUSION The poem, therefore, starting from what could be mis-read as an appalling jokiness about the image, asserts that even this is a visible manifestation of the presence of Christ, who shares in the suffering and proclaims his pacifist values on the battlefield. These values remain the 'truth untold', whatever by now is Owen's human-ist belief.

Notes

1 *The Collected Poems of Wilfred Owen*, ed. C. Day-Lewis (London: Chatto and Windus, 1963), p. 126.
2 *The War Poems of Wilfred Owen*, ed. Jon Stallworthy (London: Chatto and Windus, 1994), pp. 74–5.

Part Four

Reference Section

Biographical list

BELLOC, HILAIRE (1870–1953) Poet, historian, Catholic propagandist, traveller, journalist. He appealed to Owen, probably because he was half-French. Wilfred had two books by Belloc in his library, *Gems from Hilaire Belloc* and *Esto Perpetua* (1911 edition), and had clearly read others. In June 1915 Owen, while living in France, told his mother that he thought much of Belloc (*CL* p. 342). He then quoted from an essay in *Hills and the Sea* (1906) describing military training. (I give the passage in full: Owen only quotes the last sentence, but it is the sentence before which seems to encapsulate what Owen was to do.) Belloc explains all the chores he – a former gentleman – could now do:

> I knew all about my horses; I could sweep, wash, make a bed, clean kit, cook a little, tidy a stable, turn to entrenching for emplacement, take a place at lifting a gun or changing a wheel. I took change with a gunner, and could point well. And all this was not learnt save under a grinding pressure of authority and harshness, without which in one's whole life I suppose one would never properly have learnt a half of these things – at least not to do them so readily, or in such unison, or on so definite a plan. But (what will seem astonishing to our critics and verbalists), with all this there increased the power, or perhaps it was but the desire, to express the greatest thoughts – newer and keener things. I began to understand De Vigny when he wrote, 'If any man despairs of becoming a poet, let him carry his pack and march in the ranks'.
> 'The First Day's March'

Belloc also contributed to the British war effort by writing rather simplistic newspaper articles based upon ignorance of the facts. These were regularly caricatured in the *Wipers Times*, for example:

> By Belary Helloc
> In this article I wish to show plainly that under existing conditions, everything points to a speedy disintegration of the enemy. We will first of all take the effect of war on the male population of Germany. Firstly let us take as our figures 12,000,000 as the total fighting population of Germany. Of these 8,000,000 are killed or being killed hence we have 4,000,000 remaining . . .

By a further process of elimination he finds that there are only sixteen men left on the Western Front.

BLUNDEN, EDMUND (1896–1974) Born in London, Blunden grew up in a village in Kent. He was educated at Christ's Hospital; then entered the Army in 1914. He was a Lieutenant in the Royal Sussex Regiment in France 1916–18; awarded the Military Cross in November 1916. He describes his war experiences fully in *Undertones of War* (1928), which has a batch of his important war poems printed at the back. The gentle title and the occasional touches of humour reminiscent of Charles Lamb never quite conceal the horror hidden behind the understatement. In Chapters 9 and 10 he describes the Somme front at Beaumont Hamel in October/November 1916, i.e. just before Owen arrived at the scene.

After the war he attended Oxford University with Robert Graves, and so came to know the members of his circle:

> Siegfried, when literary editor of the *Herald*, had been among the first to recognise him as a poet, and now I was helping him to get his *Waggoner* through the press. Edmund had war-shock as badly as myself, and we would talk each other into an almost hysterical state about the trenches.[1]

He taught in Japan and Oxford, and later was Professor of English at Hong Kong. He published *The Waggoner* (1920), *The Shepherd* (1922), and *English Poems* (1925); in these poems, which often deal with English rural scenes, there is still the sense that he has been spared to write on these matters, and the Great War is never far away. He edited a collection of Owen's poems in 1931, contributing a valuable memoir, often based on sources which have not come down to us.

BOTTOMLEY, HORATIO (1860–1933) A notorious journalist and financial operator. He founded *John Bull* in 1906. Liberal MP 1906–12. He became bankrupt, but rehabilitated himself by posing as a patriot during the war. His propaganda of hatred was usually quite obnoxious, but he was widely known. Independent MP 1918–22. Imprisoned 1922–27. Owen attacks him in his letters.

BROCK, CAPTAIN A.J. (1879–1947) A Scottish doctor who had trained at Edinburgh University. Owen's psychiatrist at Craiglockhart Hospital, Edinburgh; he believed in rehabilitating the victims of shell-shock with a programme of directed activities, known as 'ergotherapy'. This included involvement in the local community. He also believed in *facing* the obsessive nightmares in the minds of his patients, and Owen was encouraged to write about his dreams in order to take control of them. This may be the origin of 'Dulce et Decorum Est' as well as various strange minor poems about death and horror. Brock was also President of the Field Club, which reawakened Owen's interest in biology. Brock wrote about his theories in 'The Re-education of the Adult: The Neurasthenic in War and Peace', *Sociological Review*, x (Summer 1918); and in *Health and Conduct* (1923).

BROOKE, RUPERT CHAWNER (1887–1915) Born at Rugby. Educated at Rugby School and at King's College, Cambridge. While writing a study of Webster's plays for his fellowship, he lived at Grantchester, where he was visited by Virginia Woolf and other members of the Bloomsbury group. He welcomed the first Post-Impressionist exhibition to be mounted in England. His sense of humour as well as his awareness of seventeenth-century poetry (before T.S. Eliot made it popular) may be seen in this extract from a review of H.J. Grierson's *Poems of John Donne*:

> One of the most remarkable of the English pictures in the recent post-Impressionist exhibition depicts John Donne arriving in Heaven. 'I don't know who John Donne is,' a sturdy member of the public was lately heard to remark in front of it, 'but he seems to be getting there!' Unconsciously, he summed up Donne's recent history . . .

Travelled in Germany and later in America and the Pacific. Died of blood-poisoning *en route* to Gallipoli in 1915. Buried on Skyros. A contemporary account of his death may be found in a letter from Charles Lister, son of Lord Ribblesdale, to Reverend Ronald Knox:

> HOOD BATTALION, B.M.E.F.
> Rupert Brooke died of blood-poisoning caused by a germ called the *pneumo coccus*. He had been rather pulled down at Port Said and suffered from the sea, so the *p.c.* had a favourable field to work in. There was no doubt as to his fate; he died within twenty-four hours of the ill making itself manifest. He was buried in an olive-grove hidden in a ravine thick with scrub that runs from a stony mountain down to the sea. The grave is under an olive-tree that bends over it like a weeping angel. A sad end to such dazzling purity of mind and work, clean cut, classical, and unaffected all the time like his face, unfurrowed or lined by cares. And the eaglet had begun to beat his wings and soar. Perhaps the Island of Achilles is in some respects a suitable resting-place for those bound for the plains of Troy.[2]

This kind of classical eulogy helps to bolster and explain the right-wing legend. The description of his face and its apparent calm shows how much he had suppressed or, alternatively, his relief from having escaped from the pressures of his private life into public activity. One had to wait until Christopher Hassall's biography of the 1960s to get a fuller and more truthful account of his life.

Published *Poems* (1911) and posthumously *1914 and Other Poems*. Many of his poems and humorous verses such as 'The Old Vicarage, Grantchester':

> Stands the church clock at ten to three
> And is there honey still for tea?

became well-known because they were printed in the *Georgian Poetry* anthologies. The war sonnets first appeared in *New Numbers* in December 1914.

CLAUSEN, SIR GEORGE (1852–1944) His name indicates Danish descent. He began as a builder's draughtsman, and then attended the National Art School, South Kensington. For a short time he worked in Paris; his approach to subject matter was much influenced by Bastien-Lepage, so that he painted landscape and agricultural scenes. He exhibited at the Royal Academy from 1876 to 1943, and was elected Royal Academician in 1908. His most famous war painting was *In the Gun factory at Woolwich Arsenal 1918*. In the 1920s he designed railway posters, and painted a mural in St Stephen's Hall in the Palace of Westminster.

GIBSON, WILFRID WILSON (1878–1962) Usually referred to as W.W. Gibson; he came from Hexham in Northumberland, and became a social worker in the East End of London from 1912. He was one of Rupert Brooke's circle, and was known as 'Wibson'. He knew Edward Marsh and contributed to *Georgian Poetry*; he also knew Harold Monro and had been an early tenant at the Poetry Bookshop. Wilfred owned his volume *Battle* (1915), which describes trench experiences of 1914 – 15; but these now seem not to have been his own. He enlisted in 1917 and served as a loader and packer in the Royal Army Service Corps; his point of view and his sympathies are with the ordinary private soldier. Gibson published his *Collected Poems 1905–1925* in 1926.

GRAVES, ROBERT VON RANKE (1895–1985) Educated at Charterhouse. Served throughout the war, at one point being badly injured and reported dead; letters sent to him in France were returned with the inscription 'Died of wounds – present location uncertain'. His early poems appeared in *Over the Brazier* (1916), *Goliath and David* (1916), and *Fairies and Fusiliers* (1917), the last of which Owen possessed. His autobiography, *Goodbye to All That* (1929), contains one of the most vivid accounts of the Great War; it ran to many editions and there are slight alterations between them, as Graves made mistakes and was adept in giving offence. Therefore, generally speaking, Graves's statements about Owen are to be received with caution. In later life

Graves became famous as a novelist, a love poet and a writer on classical themes.

GUNSTON, LESLIE (1895–1988) Wilfred Owen's first cousin. For a time Owen was very close to him; they competed in writing sonnets on such subjects as 'Happiness', 'Golden Hair', and 'Sunrise'. He was excused war service because of a mitral murmur, and worked in a YMCA hut as his contribution to the war effort. He published *The Nymph and Other Poems* (1917) at his own expense, but it was not a success; after the war he became an architect, and designed the Reading War Memorial.

JOERGENS, OLWEN A. (1896–?) The daughter of a neighbour of the Gunstons at Reading. Owen met her on 15 October 1915, but does not seem to have liked her much (*CL* p. 464). She joined the two cousins in a poetry group; they competed in the composition of poems on set subjects. One of these was 'The End', which, though it was his own poem, Wilfred said was in her style. She published *The Woman and the Sage and other Poems* in 1916.

KIPLING, RUDYARD (1865–1936) Poet and storyteller. One of the few poets to have celebrated the feelings of the ordinary private soldier. His son was killed at the Battle of Loos in 1915; his poems about the war were often angry and bitter. After the war he wrote the official history of the Irish Guards, which had been his son's regiment (this has recently been reprinted). Owen refers to him four times in the letters, mainly in connection with a project to translate some of Kipling's works into French. But there is no quotation, no sense that Owen is familar with his poetry at all.

LYTTON, NEVILLE (born *c*. 1875) Artist and war correspondent in the Great War; mentioned in Blunden's *Undertones of War*. Painted the murals in the Victory Hall at Balcombe, Sussex.

NICHOLS, ROBERT (1893–1944) Educated at Winchester College and at Oxford. He joined the Royal Field Artillery and served from October 1914 to August 1916. He saw the Somme battle, but was found to be suffering from shell-shock after a few weeks in the front line. He was found a safe job thereafter with the Ministry of Information and was sent to America, where he gave readings and lectures on his experiences; no slur is intended, but one contrasts what happened to Owen. A protégé of Edward Marsh, he contributed to *Georgian Poetry* and published two volumes during the war: *Invocation* (1915) and *Ardours and Endurances* (1917). As he was a friend of Robert Graves and Sassoon, Owen took the trouble to acquire the latter volume;

Nichols is discussed in Graves's correspondence with Owen, but it is not clear whether they actually met. After the war he became Professor of English at Tokyo 1921–24 , and wrote plays and novels.

POPE, JESSIE (died 1941) Born in Leicester. Educated at North London Collegiate School. Prolific and popular journalist, and author of children's books. Her recruiting poems during the Great War were famous, e.g. 'The Call':

> Who's for the trench –
> Are you, my laddie?

and provoked Owen into replying with 'Dulce et Decorum Est', which contains withering satirical intent. The poem was originally dedicated to her and she may be presumed to be 'My friend' in line 25. During the war she published *Jessie Pope's War Poems* (1915), *More War Poems* (1915) and *Simple Rhymes for Stirring Times* (1916). See *Scars Upon my Heart,* selected by Catherine Reilly.

ROSS, ROBERT BALDWIN (1869–1918) Friend of Oscar Wilde, he was an art-dealer and critic; he had become an arbiter of elegance, though of course he retained the attitudes of the 'nineties'. He was also a patron of younger writers. Sassoon introduced Owen to him and they met on 9 November 1917. Through him Owen met H.G. Wells and Arnold Bennett. Died 5 October 1918, and this was mentioned several times in Owen's final letters.

SASSOON, SIEGFRIED (1886–1967) Educated at Marlborough and Clare College, Cambridge. A country gentleman. Saw the first day on the Somme, i.e. 1 July 1916. Later wounded. In July 1917 he made a famous protest against the war, and threw his Military Cross into the mouth of the Mersey River; sent to Craiglockhart Hospital in Edinburgh and treated by W.H.R. Rivers; see his autobiographical trilogy, gathered together as *The Complete Memoirs of George Sherston,* and Pat Barker's recent novels.

SCOTT MONCRIEFF, CHARLES KENNETH (1889–1930) Poet and translator. Educated at Winchester and Edinburgh University. Joined up in August 1914; Captain and Military Cross. When Wilfred met him – at Robert Graves's wedding – he had been wounded and was working in London. As a staff officer at the War Office he was able to recommend instructors for trainee battalions; such a position was found for Robert Graves. Scott Moncrieff was greatly taken with Owen and at one stage Wilfred was encouraged to think that a similar post might be found for him. After the war Scott Moncrieff became famous as the translator of Proust.

SIMS, CHARLES (1873–1928) Painter. Studied in London and Paris. Exhibited at Royal Academy from 1893. Famous for outdoor scenes, later became known as a symbolist. *The Fountain* and *The Wood beyond the World* were purchased by Tate Gallery. Royal Academician in 1915. Official war artist in France 1918. Keeper of the Royal Academy Schools 1920–26. He seems to have been permanently affected by his son's death in 1915 and by his experiences in France; he committed suicide in 1928. His book *Picture Making* appeared in 1934.

SITWELL, OSBERT (1892–1969) Educated at Eton. Served in Grenadier Guards. Captain; fought at Battle of Loos 1915. Then invalided out. With his sister Edith and brother Sacheverell he was an advocate of a cliquy Modernism. Friendly with Sassoon and therefore introduced to Owen.

SORLEY, CHARLES HAMILTON (1895–1915) Born in Aberdeen. In 1900 his father became a professor of philosophy at Cambridge; but Sorley seems to retain a kind of Scottish no-nonsense view of the world. He lived at Chesterton Lane, Cambridge, and was educated at King's College Choir School and Marlborough College. He liked running in the rain, an activity commemorated in the much anthologised poem, 'The Song of the Ungirt Runners'. He said 'Man is not himself unless he is muddy'. From January to August 1914 he took the best part of a year out and went to learn German in Germany. He stayed with a family in Schwerin in Mecklenburg, and then in the summer term attended the University of Jena. In July he embarked on a walking tour of the Moselle valley with a friend; as they 'swung into Neumagen' one evening, they met a 'little crooked old fellow' who told them the war had begun:

> His little face was lit with a wild uncertain excitement he had not known since 1870, and he advanced towards us waving his stick and yelling at us 'Der Krieg ist los, Junge,' just as we might be running to watch a football match and he was come to tell us we must hurry up for the game had begun.

In an extraordinary sequence of events Sorley was first imprisoned at Trier on 2 August, then released after a rumour that England had declared war on Russia. He returned via Liège and arrived back in Cambridge on 6 August. He enlisted immediately without any hesitation over the fact that he was to fight his new German friends. He wrote an astonishing sonnet 'To Germany' at about this time which is remarkable in that it shows no patriotic fervour and is full of sympathy for the German position. In late 1915 he was killed at the Battle of Loos. Robert Graves wrote an odd poem about him which is not easy to find; it is called 'Sorley's Weather' because of

Sorley's insistence that rain is the best weather to be out in.

TAGORE, SIR RABINDRANATH (1861–1941) Poet of the Bengali literary revival; he translated his own poems into English. His work was promoted by Yeats and in 1913 he received the Nobel Prize for Literature. Owen mentions him for the first time in 1915.

TAILHADE, LAURENT (1854–1919) A prolific French writer, and friend of Verlaine. Wilfred Owen encountered him in August 1914 at Bagnères; he was the first poet Owen had met. Sassoon says that Owen showed his early verses to Tailhade. He corresponded with Owen and met him again in Paris; it is possible that he influenced Owen with his pacifist ideas, though he abandoned them himself.

TONKS, SIR HENRY (1862–1937) Painter and teacher. Slade Professor 1917–30. He was qualified in medicine, and was asked to document the effects of plastic surgery on war victims.

VERNÈDE, R.E. (1875–1917) A Londoner, he was educated at St Paul's School and Oxford. A novelist. Enlisted in the 9th Royal Fusiliers, September 1914. Wounded at the Battle of the Somme in 1916. Killed in action on 9 April 1917. His *War Poems and Other Verses* were published in 1917; Wilfred owned a copy.

WIGAN, REV. HERBERT (1862–1947) He had been Chaplain at Bloxham School 1891–99, and curate at Sonning 1903–4. In 1904 he became vicar of Dunsden, near Reading. Originally a Tractarian, he had literary connections which at first impressed Owen – 'He is a sixth cousin of the great William Morris!'. Though Wilfred realised that all this had long evaporated and that the vicar was now an Evangelical with a taste for antique furniture, some things do seem to have rubbed off, in spite of their estrangement when Owen left the vicarage. It is ironical that in Scarborough Owen too collected antique furniture and various poems do show an interest in church ceremonial.

Notes

1 Robert Graves, *Goodbye to All That* (London: Cape, 1931), pp. 358–9.
2 Lord Ribblesdale, *Charles Lister: Letters and Recollections* (London, T. Fisher Unwin, 1917), pp. 164–5.

Gazetteer

England

Berkshire:

READING As a boy Owen had seen the Museum, looked at Roman remains from Silchester and visited the Huntley and Palmer Biscuit Factory. He also went to the cinema: West's Picture Palace at 33 West Street. In June 1913 he stayed at 67 South Street. He visited SILCHESTER in August 1910.

Cheshire:

BROXTON Wilfred stayed in a cottage there with his mother in 1903 or 1904. Wilfred said afterwards that it was here that he first felt the vocation to be a poet.

Cumbria:

KESWICK Wilfred attended the Keswick Convention in 1912. As this was a summer school, the religious students lived in tents which were situated 1½ miles from town on the Penrith Road. Although Owen did not at first warm to the Lake District scenery, he later climbed Latrigg, and visited Castle Head and Friar's Crag.

Devonshire:

TEIGNMOUTH Visited by Wilfred in 1911 and 1913. He found the house where Keats had lived in 1818, now 20 Northumberland Place. See letter and poem 'Sonnet, written at Teignmouth, on a pilgrimage to Keats's House'.

TORQUAY Wilfred and Harold stayed at 264 Union Street in August 1910, and from there visited Plymouth. They stayed again in April 1911. In 1913 Wilfred convalesced after his illness at 18 Belle Vue Crescent, Chelston.

Essex:

GIDEA PARK, ROMFORD From 15 November 1915 Wilfred was in camp at Hare Hall. See B. Evans, *Romford, Collier Row and Gidea Park* (Phillimore, 1994) for a good selection of photographs of the camp during the Great War. The poet Edward Thomas was at the same camp as a map-reading instructor; this seems to be the origin of his famous poems listing Essex place-names.

Hampshire:

ALDERSHOT Wilfred was posted to Talavera Barracks in July 1916 for a musketry course. In August he was at Farnborough.

NETLEY In June 1917 Owen was temporarily a patient at the Royal Victoria Hospital, Netley. This was demolished in 1966.

WINCHESTER Leslie Gunston worked in the YMCA Hut at Hazeley Down. Wilfred visited him there in 1918; he spent the afternoon in the cathedral.

Lancashire:

FLEETWOOD While in charge of firing parties from November to 8 December 1916 Owen stayed at 111 Bold Street.

London:

WIMBLEDON The Owens occasionally visited the Gunstons, who were living at Alpina, 3 Clement Road from 1906 to 1908. Leslie was at King's College School, Wimbledon, and sometimes saw Swinburne crossing the Common; he lived at The Pines in Putney. In September 1911 Wilfred Owen lived in a room at 'Glenmore', 38 Worple Road, while taking his London Matriculation Exam. From this base he visited Keats' House, Keats' Grove, Hampstead, and the British Museum, where he made a special effort to see MSS of Keats. He also went to the Tate Gallery, the National Portrait Gallery and Hampton Court.

In 1915 Owen found himself at various hotels while visiting the city; in October after enlisting in the Artists' Rifles in Duke's Road he stayed at a pension called Les Lilas, 54 Tavistock Square. The soldiers drilled in Cartwright Gardens. The Poetry Bookshop, which he stayed at in February 1916, was at 35 Devonshire Street, now Boswell Street, Theobalds Road, but the actual building is no longer there.

In late 1917 and 1918 Wilfred moved in more elevated circles. He lunched at the Reform Club on several occasions and attended Robert Graves's wedding at St James's, Piccadilly.

Merseyside:

BIRKENHEAD Tom Owen's first post here was as Stationmaster at Woodside Station. In 1898 the family's first house was at 14 Willmer Road, Tranmere; then they moved to 7 Elm Grove, and finally in the winter of that year to 51 Milton Road. The Birkenhead Institute was in Whetstone Lane; Wilfred attended Sunday School at Christ Church.

SOUTHPORT From October 1916 Owen attended courses at Southport, staying first at 168a Lord Street; then he moved to the Queen's Hotel, where he stayed when not occupied at Fleetwood.

Oxfordshire:

DUNSDEN is a village about two miles north-east of Caversham, the northern transfluminar suburb of Reading. The church (All Saints) is amalgamated with Shiplake for pastoral purposes. Tom, Susan and Mary Owen lie in Dunsden Churchyard now. Wilfred first visited the vicarage in June 1911, and lived there from 12 October 1911 till 7 February 1913.

KIDMORE END is in the same area. The Gunston's family home was called Alpenrose; they moved there in 1908, and members of the Owen family visited them there. It was a smallholding with about eight acres of land.

In 1912 Wilfred also visited Sonning, Caversham, Wargrave, Wallingford and Mapledurham. He attended a meeting at Henley Town Hall (built 1900–1).

OXFORD Wilfred Owen's personal library, more or less complete, is preserved in the English Faculty Library. There is a checklist of its contents at the back of JS. The library also has a collection of MSS, photographs, and other personalia.

Shropshire:

OSWESTRY Wilfred Owen is honoured in the town of his birth with a metal plaque on a slate bench near St Oswald's Church. This is inscribed with his dates and two complete poems: 'Anthem for Doomed Youth' and 'Futility', together with his monogram and the badge of the Artists' Rifles. Plas Wilmot, the house where Wilfred was born, is in the Croeswylan district south of Oswestry. (The 1897 bill of sale is reproduced on p. 12 of JS.) Take the Morda Road from the centre of the town then turn left into Western Road; Plas Wilmot is just after Wilmot Drive. It is a private house and is not open to visitors. Further to the east in the neighbourhood of Oswestry College lie Wilfred Owen Road, Wilfred Owen Avenue and Wilfred Owen Close. Wilfred also attended a course at Oswestry camp in 1916.

SHREWSBURY For a short time in 1897 the family lived at Canon Street, where Harold Owen was born. When they returned from Birkenhead the Owens lived at 1 Cleveland Place, Underdale Road from 1907 to 1910; the Owen grandparents lived at Hawthorn Villa in Underdale Road itself. Then from 1910 onwards the family established themselves permanently at 'Mahim', 71 Monkmoor Road, a newish house built in 1905. The house has a plaque recording Wilfred Owen's residence. Wilfred's room was in the attic storey. These houses are situated in a small estate east of the river, and north of the area associated with the Abbey. The house was conveniently placed for the father's work; the family sometimes attended church at St Giles' Church, St Julian's Church, or the Abbey and occasionally at Holy Trinity, Uffington, a village much further to the east.

The Technical School was conveniently near for Wilfred on the east side of English Bridge. He was a part-time pupil teacher at Wyle Cop School in 1910 and then full-time for the summer term in 1911.

From his home Owen frequently made excursions to Haughmond Hill; in the *Walks in Shropshire* series there is a Wilfred Owen walk, which takes you there and includes other sites. This may be obtained from the Tourist Information Centres in Shropshire, or from the Publications Officer, Shropshire Books, The Old School, Preston Street, Shrewsbury SY2 5NY.

The Wilfred Owen Association is a charity based in Shrewsbury and has been responsible for establishing the local memorials. Information can be obtained from the Membership Secretary, 17 Belmont, Shrewsbury, SY1 1TE. The new memorial to Wilfred Owen is in the grounds of Shrewsbury Abbey. It is in the form of a tunnel entrance (see illustration).

URICONIUM The Roman town, also called Wroxeter, is about five miles east of Shrewsbury. There are various references to Owen's visits in *CL*. See Owen's early poem 'Uriconium – an Ode'.

Surrey:

WITLEY, NEAR GUILDFORD After being commissioned in June 1916 Wilfred was posted to Milford Camp, which was in fact some way from Milford. He visited Guildford and Godalming by bicycle.

Yorkshire:

RIPON In 1918 Owen was assigned to the military camp to the west of the town, but after a while he found a room at 7 Borage Lane (now renumbered and respelt as 23 Borrage Lane). From here he visited Ripon cathedral and Fountains Abbey.

SCARBOROUGH Wilfred first saw Scarborough in 1905 when the family went there for a holiday, staying with Cousin May, a distant relative of Susan Owen. Clarence Gardens Hotel (now the Clifton Hotel) is on the edge of the North Cliff.

Memorial to Wilfred Owen at Shrewsbury by Paul de Mouchaux. The inscription reads 'I am the enemy you killed, my friend.'
Photo: Roger White

Scotland

EDINBURGH Craiglockhart Hydro. Outside the town to the south-west is a large building which was constructed as a Hydropathic Establishment beween 1877 and 1880; in 1916 it became a military hospital run by the Red Cross. Sassoon called it Slateford as this was the name of the nearest station. It is now in educational use. Owen taught at Tynecastle Secondary School nearby.

KELSO In 1912 Wilfred stayed at Pringle Bank, Kelso; he saw Abbotsford and Flodden Field.

Wales

Although he prided himself on his distant Welsh ancestry, Owen's visits to Wales were only in childhood when he stayed with a school-friend Alec Paton, at Glan Clwyd, Rhewl, near Ruthin, North Wales.

Ireland

In 1902 the family went to Waterford for a holiday and stayed in rented rooms at Tramore, a holiday resort on the south coast.

141

France

ABBEVILLE Ancient town at the mouth of the Somme, where Wilfred took a course in transport duties in February 1917. He tells his mother that he made a study of the town when he was fourteen, presumably from a Ruskinian point of view, and so is familiar with its landmarks. This would not be possible today as the interior of the church and much of the town were destroyed in the Second World War.

BAGNÈRES-DE-BIGORRE Hautes Pyrénées. A holiday resort with baths and a casino where Wilfred attended a lecture. He spent a month in the summer of 1914 at a villa called Castel Lorenzo.

BEAUMONT HAMEL A small village north of Albert, in the valley of the River Ancre. During the Battle of the Somme it was a German fortress and held out until November 1916; but their forces were still entrenched in the general area of Beaumont Hamel when Owen arrived in January 1917. A large section of the trenches from the Great War has been preserved to the west of the village – see the Newfoundland Memorial Park. There are a large number of British memorials and cemeteries in this area, commemorating the Battle of the Somme.

BORDEAUX In 1913–15 Owen stayed at a wide variety of addresses (which can be found in *CL*) while teaching private pupils and giving classes at the Berlitz School (at 46 Cours Intendance). There have been so many changes of street names that it is not easy to identify these. Mérignac, where the de la Touche family lived, is some miles west of the main town and is where the airport is now situated. The house where Owen stayed has been demolished.

BREST Visited for holidays with his father in 1908 and 1909.

CORBIE Village near Amiens on the Canal de la Somme, near Gailly where Wilfred was treated in the Casualty Clearing Station. Owen visited the 'great Gothic church' and attended vespers. On 15 September 1918 he rejoined his regiment here.

ÉTAPLES This was the famous transit camp described by Graves etc., and contained the Bull-ring for training. Wilfred passed through here on both his tours of duty in France. His famous description of the atmosphere of the camp in early 1917 may be found in a reminiscence of 31 December 1917:

> It seemed neither France nor England, but a kind of paddock where the beasts are kept a few days before the shambles. I heard the revelling of the Scotch troops, who are now dead, and who knew they would be dead.

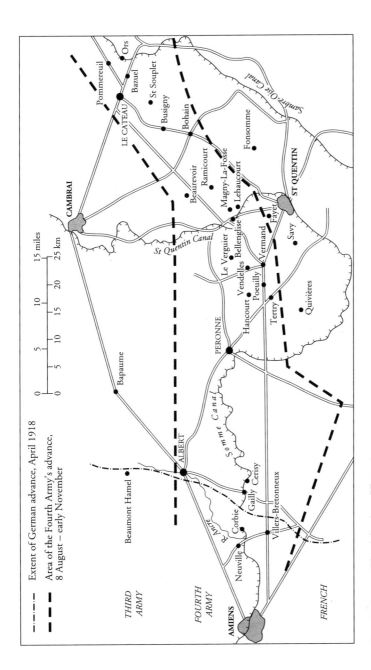

Fourth Army: 'The March to Victory'
Source: *Wilfred Owen: The Last Year* (Dominic Hibberd). By permission of Constable Publishers

Wilfred Owen's grave at Ors

... But chiefly I thought of the very strange look on all faces in that camp; an incomprehensible look, which a man will never see in England, though wars should be in England; nor can it be seen in any battle. But only in Etaples.

It was not despair, or terror, it was more terrible than terror, for it was a blindfold look, and without expression, like a dead rabbit's. (*CL* p. 521)

ÉTRETAT Seaside town on the Channel coast near Le Havre, where Wilfred was looked after by American nurses in June 1917.

ORS A small village near Le Cateau. Owen's grave is in the British section of the Communal cemetery near the station. There are comparatively few graves, and the association with the French civil cemetery is reassuring.

ST QUENTIN A large industrial town on the Somme, the object of the attack in which Owen was involved in April 1917. He saw 'the glorious prospect of the cathedral Town just below us, glittering with the morning. With glasses I could easily make out the general architecture of the cathedral: so I have told you how near we have got' (*CL* p. 450). It was not liberated until 1 October 1918 when Owen was fighting to the north of the town. It has a large Gothic church. The A26 motorway runs roughly along the line of the British positions in early 1917.

Further reading

Poems

The publication history of the poems has been discussed earlier. All the earlier editions have their importance and are worth consulting for more than just historical points, but all are out of print. (Note, however, that Sassoon's text of 1920 has been reprinted by the Imperial War Museum, ed. Martin Taylor, 1990.) All are now superseded by Jon Stallworthy, ed., *Wilfred Owen: The Complete Poems and Fragments*, 2 vols (London: Chatto and Windus, Hogarth Press, and Oxford University Press, 1983). A subsequent paperback edition includes most of the material usually considered important: see Jon Stallworthy, ed., *The War Poems of Wilfred Owen* (London: Chatto and Windus, 1994). See also Jon Silkin, ed., *The War Poems: Wilfred Owen* (London: Sinclair-Stevenson, 1994) for this editor's perceptive humanist readings of the poems.

Letters

These are available in *Wilfred Owen: Collected Letters*, edited by Harold Owen and John Bell (London, New York and Toronto: Oxford University Press, 1967). (Harold Owen was Wilfred's younger brother: see further below.) This mass of letters – there are nearly 700 of them – provide vivid evidence of Owen's experiences and what he thought of them. But 631 of the letters are addressed to members of his family and of these 554 are written to his mother. What a son would wish to convey, and what he would inevitably conceal from his mother, must be borne in mind while considering these. On the other hand it is clear that he used letters as a form of diary and asked his mother to keep them for future reference. He sometimes made drafts of the letters before sending them out in final form; and there is a reference to their being typed up and circulated, so that their public nature is a conscious purpose of the writer. On the other hand Harold Owen did suppress certain passages, which cannot now be recovered. N.B. This edition does have some errors, especially dating. A new paperback edition is promised for autumn 1998.

Owen's life: biographies and memoirs

A PRELIMINARY NOTE OF CAUTION, FOLLOWING ON FROM THE ABOVE. A great deal is known about Owen's life, including a lot of day-by-day

'fascinating detail'. This is both helpful and unhelpful; detail is always 'fascinating', but the closely knitted web of local and actual
reference may obscure what is going on under the surface, i.e. slower
and deeper currents. There is also the question of conscious or
unconscious bias in the principal sources. This includes the letters –
already discussed above – and the poems. Of course there is biographical evidence in the poetry, but it will not do to use the poems
as if they were all 'confessional', however 'sincere' they may appear
to be; this is to ignore the fictive elements, such as the retelling of
dreams. Even in poems which rely on experience one must bear in
mind the re-arrangement of life by memory, and the way in which
poets incorporate other people's experiences as their own. Though
some poems have sections of reportage, it would be foolish to treat
them as newspaper accounts or straightforward historical documents.
(This kind of naivety has bedevilled biographical work on Wordsworth,
Keats and Shelley, for example.) For the early years we have the autobiography of Harold Owen, *Journey from Obscurity*, 3 vols (Oxford:
Oxford University Press, 1963–65), followed by *Aftermath* in 1970.
This is required reading, the first volume at any rate. Nobody would
wish to lose any of the anecdotes it contains, but it is locked into the
point of view of a member of the family who is desperate to present
his elder brother as a heroic figure.

In the standard biography – Jon Stallworthy, *Wilfred Owen: A Biography* (London: Chatto/Oxford University Press, 1974) – a careful
balance has been achieved; there are also well-selected and relevant
illustrations. A new paperback edition is announced for the autumn
of 1998. However, as with all complete lives of Owen (or similar
short-lived subjects, as has often been pointed out), the need to bulk
out the account of his earlier years so that due proportion is observed has produced works in which most time is spent on the youth-
ful and formative stages and not enough on the main creative period
at the end of his life. For an attempt to redress this see Dominic
Hibberd, *Wilfred Owen: The Last Year* (London: Constable, 1992). The
book contains fresh material and interpretations, together with a
wealth of new illustrations. Hibberd had previously produced a complete survey of Owen's life and work in *Owen the Poet* (London:
Macmillan, 1986), in which the stress is on the poetry rather than
the purely biographical material.

Memoirs

For source material and contemporary accounts see first Siegfried
Sassoon, *The Complete Memoirs of George Sherston* (London: Faber and
Faber, 1972) and *Siegfried's Journey 1916–1920* (London: Faber and

Reference section

Faber, 1945). Sassoon's diaries are available in *Siegfried Sassoon: Diaries 1915–1918*, ed. Rupert Hart-Davis (London: Faber and Faber, 1983).

Osbert Sitwell has already been quoted (see p. 35). The source is Osbert Sitwell, *Noble Essences or Courteous Revelations* (London: Macmillan, 1950). Most other contemporary reminiscence was sifted and used in Blunden's 'Memoir', attached to his collection of Owen's poems and the Day-Lewis edition. Hibberd has also interviewed those remaining persons who had known Owen and used their reminiscences in his books.

Criticism

The first monograph was written by D.S.R. Welland, *Wilfred Owen: A Critical Study* (London: Chatto and Windus, 1960) and remains invaluable. The most important recent book is Douglas Kerr, *Wilfred Owen's Voices: Language and Community* (Oxford: Clarendon Press, 1993). Most other useful criticism is in periodicals or in some of the books listed above and below.

Poetry of the First World War

An enormous amount of verse was written: see Catherine Reilly, *English Poetry of the First World War: A Bibliography* (London: George Prior, 1978). Some libraries, e.g. Birmingham Public Library, have interesting collections of contemporary material. It is always worth asking in older libraries if they have a special collection. Frequently local parents put together a memorial volume for their son, or left papers; these often include poems.

At the time a number of collections appeared, e.g. Galloway Kyle, ed., *Songs of the Fighting Men* (London: Erskine Macdonald, 1916) and *More Songs by the Fighting Men* (London: Erskine Macdonald, 1917). Generally the theme is avowedly patriotic, but it is important to note that criticism of the war was allowed from the earliest days. Commemorative volumes appeared in the 1920s. During the 1960s attempts were made to comb through the mass of material, but these were curiously similar in their editorial premisses, which were those of teachers of English. The compilers were constrained by good taste and post-Leavisite respect for the integrity of the poem. They went for short and pointed statements and excluded sentimental twaddle of which there is a great deal. Secondly, they wished to interpret the war in terms of the poetry, and assumed that the poems would fit their schemas; others simply printed the poems in alphabetical order of authors' names. In neither case were they really looking for a historical survey of the poetry, but trying to sort out what was now worth reading. With these caveats, see the following good anthologies: Brian Gardner, ed., *Up the Line to Death* (London: Methuen, 1964), I.M. Parsons, ed., *Men Who March Away* (London: Chatto and Windus, 1966), Maurice Hussey, ed., *Poetry of the First World War* (London: Longman, 1967) and later Jon Silkin, ed., *Penguin Book of First World War Poetry* (Harmondsworth: Penguin, 1979).

Catherine Reilly, ed., *Scars Upon My Heart: Women's Poetry and Verse of the First World War* (London: Virago, 1981) was an important change of emphasis; by including the word 'verse' in the title she exemplified the librarian's rather than the English teacher's approach, and unearthed some surprising sentiments which did not fit received opinion:

> Oh it's you that have the luck, out there in blood and muck:
>   You were born beneath a kindly star;
> All we dreamt, I and you, you can really go and do,
>   And I can't, the way things are.
>   Rose Macaulay, 'Many Sisters to Many Brothers' (1915)

As Reilly points out, this contains an important testimony in spite of its naive sentiments, yet could not have been written after 1915, when the slaughter became so unbearable. The way was now open to an anthology based on historical principles rather than good taste, and a start on this has been provided by Dominic Hibberd and John Onions, eds, *Poetry of the Great War: An Anthology* (Basingstoke: Macmillan, 1986). Here, for example, is a whole section of poems about Christ, which show that Owen was not unique in his 'identification' of the soldiers with the religious figure, but then open up the possibility that Owen knew this full well and deliberately used the cliché for his own purposes.

Criticism of Great War poetry must therefore be evaluated with the same caveats as established above. Most editors and critics are looking for great poems rather than typical ones, and are usually pursuing other hares, e.g. the emergence of Modernism. But see the pioneering John H. Johnston, *English Poetry of the First World War: A Study in the Evolution of Lyric and Narrative Form* (Oxford: Oxford University Press, 1964) and Bernard Bergonzi, *Heroes' Twilight* (London: Constable, 1965). Later work includes Jon Silkin, *Out of Battle: The Poetry of the Great War* (London: Oxford University Press, 1972; London: Routledge, 1987) and Desmond Graham, *The Truth of War: Owen, Blunden and Rosenberg* (Manchester: Carcanet, 1984).

Military history

The shelves of bookshops groan with general accounts of the war, and it is an impossible task to survey them. The contemporary references for a study of Owen's last campaign are R.E. Priestley, *Breaking the Hindenburg Line* (London: T. Fisher Unwin, 1919), A. Montgomery, *The Story of the Fourth Army in the Battle of the Hundred Days* (London: Hodder and Stoughton, 1920) and there are later official histories.

Traditional narrative accounts of the war are now supplemented by the series of works by Lyn Macdonald based on oral history interviews, for example: *They called it Passchendaele* (London: Macmillan 1978) and *Somme* (London: Macmillan 1983).

Cultural history

Here the pioneering work was undoubtedly Paul Fussell, *The Great War and Modern Memory* (New York and London: Oxford University Press, 1975), which changed the direction of criticism and appreciation, in spite of some inaccuracies about English life and historical context. It was now possible to see the war as myth, and to detach the pursuit of what actually happened (political and military history) from the discussion of what was now generally received as having happened (in poetry, fiction and criticism), which became a subject of semi-sociological enquiry. An example is the history of the ideal of chivalry, pursued by Mark Girouard in *The Return to Camelot: Chivalry and the English Gentleman* (New Haven and London: Yale University Press, 1981).

The situation is further complicated and convoluted because the Great War remains a more ghastly experience than the Second World War in the people's memory, and still seems to dominate the ceremonies at the Cenotaph upon Remembrance Sunday. It remains present to many families, often in an unexpected way – see, for example, Alan Bennett's tale of *Uncle Clarence*. This persistence of memory has enabled subsequent generations, not just Great War survivors, to express themselves with some validity, especially about the mourning process. See Geoff Dyer, *The Missing of the Somme* (London: Penguin, 1995) and Jay Winter, *Sites of Memory, Sites of Mourning: The Great War in European Cultural History* (Cambridge: Cambridge University Press, 1995), which places 'Strange Meeting' in an unusual category called 'conversations with the dead'.

Creative work referring to Owen

People always used to ask why the Second World War did not produce poetry like that of the Great War, but as time goes by the question has become irrelevant. Keith Douglas, in many ways a clinical and accurate recorder of events which he allowed to speak for themselves, wrote an essay on the subject in 1943:

Why are there no poets like Owen and Sassoon who lived with
the fighting troops and wrote of their experiences while they were
enduring them?

The reasons are psychological, literary, military and strategic,
diverse. There are such poets, but they do not write. They do not
write because there is nothing new, from a soldier's point of view,
about this war except its mobile character. There are two reasons:
hell cannot be let loose twice: it was let loose in the Great War
and it is the same old hell now. The hardships, pain and boredom;
the behaviour of the living and the appearance of the dead, were
so accurately described by the poets of the Great War that every-
day on the battlefields of the western desert – and no doubt on
the Russian battlefields as well – their poems are illustrated.

This appears in Desmond Graham, ed., *Keith Douglas: A Prose Miscel-
lany* (Manchester: Carcanet Press, 1985). Nevertheless Douglas did
succeed sometimes in breaking through the reserve which constrained
his emotions. An example is 'Enfidaville', about a ruined village in
Tunisia:

In the church fallen like dancers
lie the Virgin and St. Thérèse
on little pillows of dust.
The detonations of the last few days
tore down the ornamental plasters
shivered the hands of Christ.

The men and women who moved like candles
in and out of the houses and the streets
are all gone. The white houses are bare
black cages. . . .

[He goes on to describe the desolation, but then in the last stanza]

But already they are coming back; to search
like ants, poking in the débris, finding in it
a bed or a piano and carrying it out.
Who would not love them at this minute?
I seem again to meet
The blue eyes of the images in the church.

In the next generation of poets Ted Hughes's 'Wilfred Owen's photographs', published in 1960, refers obliquely to the story of Owen's
shocking photographs of wounded soldiers. Pat Barker has produced
three novels referring to Owen and some of his contemporaries,
which form a connected trilogy. These are *Regeneration* (London: Viking, 1991; Penguin, 1992), *The Eye in the Door* (London: Viking,
1993; Penguin, 1994) and *The Ghost Road* (London: Viking, 1995).

Though the novels are connected together through a fictional character, Billy Prior, the real interest of the series is in W.H.R. Rivers (not really a psychiatrist but an anthropologist and a nerve specialist) who worked at Craiglockhart and oversees the healing and eventual recovery of his charges. (In fact Owen was placed under Dr Brock whose methods were not the same.)

Regeneration is a reconstruction of Rivers's time as a Royal Army Medical Corps doctor at Craiglockhart. Apart from various characters, whose cases illustrate the strange effects of shell-shock, the principal 'real' patient is Siegfried Sassoon; his 'progress' is charted from his famous letter of protest up to his return to duty. Owen features as a minor character and the well-known details of his poetic relation to Sassoon are sketched in rather barely; I think it is assumed that the reader will be able to flesh these out.

But several things come out which are not usually stressed. (1) That Owen's case was typical, i.e. that the prolonged experience of battle finally tipped him over into 'madness'. This state was brought about as a result of the death of comrades and literally 'triggered' by the explosion of a shell close by. (2) That Rivers was not interested in Sassoon's poetry except as a record of mad states, whereas Dr Brock seems to have been genuinely interested in Owen's. (3) All of them except Sassoon were at some point 'barking mad', so that Owen's account of his own case leaves a lot out.

A film of *Regeneration* was released in 1997.

Sebastian Faulks, *Birdsong* (London: Hutchinson, 1993; Vintage, 1994) is a much-praised novel about the Great War. While at times it seems completely out of touch with the mores and manners of the period, it feels surprisingly authentic in its narrative of battle. The final tunnelling sequences are a reworking of 'Strange Meeting'.

General index

Abbeville, 21, 142
Aldershot, 20, 138
Amiens, 22, 26, 50, 114
Ancre, River, 123, 142
Antwerp, 46, 66
Armistice Day 1918, 28, 50
Arnold, Matthew, 112
Artists' Rifles, 19, 32, 138, 139
Asquith, Herbert, 64
assonance, 33, 85, 88, 94, 98,
    104–5, 118
Athenaeum, The, 103–5
Auden, W.H., 88, 121

Bagnères-de-Bigorre, 15–16, 136,
    142
ballad-form, 89–90
Barker, Pat, 36, 134, 151–2
Baudelaire, 121
Beaumont Hamel, 20, 50, 91, 130,
    142
Belgium, 45–6, 49–50
Belloc, Hilaire, 55, 129
Bennett, Arnold, 25, 35, 134
Binyon, Laurence, 64
Birkenhead, 11, 138–9
Bloomsbury group, 65, 91
Blunden, Edmund, 130
  as war poet, 63, 69–71, 108
  'Concert Party: Busseboom',
    70–1
  editor of poems, 31, 115, 119
  Memoir of O., 33–4, 91, 148
  'Pillbox', 111
  Undertones of War, 42, 133
Boer War, 41
Bone, Muirhead, 61
Bookman, The, 31, 84, 86
Bordeaux, 14–17, 26, 41, 64, 100,
    142
botany, 12, 24
Bottomley, Horatio, 51, 53, 124,
    130

Brest, 142
Britten, Benjamin, 98
Brock, Capt. A.J., 24, 130–1, 152
Brockway, Fenner, 72
Brooke, Rupert, 65–7, 70, 131–2
Browning, Robert, 112
Broxton, 137

Cambrai, 49
Cavell, Edith, 50
Christianity,
  and war, 42–4
  O's rejection of, 13–14, 75–6,
    96, 99–100, 123–5
  rituals, 17
Churchill, W.S., 50, 65
Clausen, George, 57, 132
Coleridge, S.T., 89, 100, 105, 117
conscription, 49, 72
consonantal rhyme, *see* assonance
Coppard, George, 45
Corbie, 142
Craiglockhart Hospital, 23–5, 26,
    34, 36, 49, 70, 73, 83, 87,
    91–2, 104, 107, 111, 130,
    141, 152

Dante, 105–6
Day-Lewis, C.,
  edition of O's poems, 31, 33, 85,
    148
de la Touche family, 16, 17, 142
Douglas, Keith, 150–1
Dunsden, 12–14, 17, 26, 91,
    99–100, 136, 139

Edinburgh, 23–5, 90, 91, 130, 141
  see also Craiglockhart
elegies,
  classical, 96
  O's poems as, 81, 98
Eliot, T.S., 112, 118–19, 121
erotic poems, 22, 31, 69, 85–6

153

Romantic tradition of poetry, 12,
    33–4, 63, 82, 89, 90, 95,
    100, 105, 117
Romford, 20, 137–8
Ross, Robert, 25, 34–5, 134
Rossetti, D.G., 103
Royal Academy, 55–7, 132, 135
Russell, Bertrand, 72
Russia, 45, 49

sacrifice, in war, 42–4
St John's Gospel, 'Greater love
    . . .', 43, 75, 125
St Quentin, 22, 26, 50, 96, 145
Sambre/Oise canal, 27
Sassoon, Siegfried, 107–9, 134
    and peace party, 72–4
    at Craiglockhart, 24, 92, 107,
        141, 152
    compared to O., 118–19, 121–2
    edits O.'s poems, 30–2, 102,
        112, 114, 116, 119, 146
    helps Blunden, 130
    letters to O., 101, 104
    'Mad Jack', 108
    mental state in 1917, 36
    on 'Strange Meeting', 107
    returns to France, 76
    tutors O., 24–5, 68, 69, 71, 76,
        86, 87
    works,
        'Blighters', 51
        diary, 34, 148
        'Died of Wounds', 111
        'Does it matter . . . ?', 108
        'For the last time I say . . .',
            76
        'General, The', 69–70
        Old Huntsman, The, 107–8
        Sherston's Progress, 24, 34, 72–3,
            147
        'Sick Leave', 74
        Siegfried's Journey, 25, 34–5,
            147
Scarborough, 25–6, 30, 49, 50, 76,
    84, 119, 136, 140
'Schlieffen plan', 46
Scott Moncrieff, Charles, 32–3,
    134

Second World War, x, 34, 150–1
shell-shock *see* neurasthenia
Shelley, P.B., 13–14, 34, 98–103,
    106
Shrewsbury, 12, 26, 139–40
Sims, Charles, 55–9, 97, 135
Sitwell family, 31, 101, 110, 119
    Osbert, 35, 123, 135, 148
Somme, battle of the, 48, 142
    changed opinions, 69–70, 108,
        115
    generals' role, 49, 51
    O. in last phases, 14, 21, 26
    other poets at, 68, 130, 133,
        134, 136
    pictures, 61
Song of Solomon, The, 84
sonnet-form, 65–7, 70, 94
Sorley, Charles Hamilton, 66–8,
    70, 76, 135–6
Southport, 20, 139
Stallworthy, Jon,
    edition of O.'s poems, 30–1, 87,
        110, 114, 117, 120, 146
Swinburne, A.C., 31, 82, 113, 118,
    122, 138
Sylvester, Victor, 51

Tagore, Rabindranath, ix, 136
Tailhade, Laurent, 136
Teignmouth, 12, 137
Tennyson, Alfred, Lord, 85, 90–3,
    95, 97–8
Thomas, Edward, 137–8
Times, War Poems from The, 64
Tonks, Henry, 59–61, 136
Torquay, 14, 137
Turkey, 48

underworld locations, 100–1,
    105–6
United States, 49
Uriconium, 12, 140

Verdun, 48
Vernède, R.E., 68, 136

WAAC, 49
Wales, 141

'war artists', 54, 61, 135
War, Great,
  civilian attitudes, 50–1, 123–5
  concluding stages, 27–8
  course of, 45–50
  drift to, 41–4
  outbreak of, 15, 45–6
  remembrance of, ix–xi
  'The Sentry' and, 112
war poetry, 62–71, 85, 95, 107–9, 148–9
Wells, H.G., 25, 35, 90, 97, 134
Wheels, 31, 101, 109–10, 119–20

Wigan, Herbert, Rev., 13–14, 42, 136
Wilde, Oscar, influence of, 31, 69, 82, 118, 122
Wimbledon, 138
Winchester, 25, 57, 138
Wipers Times, The, 51, 129

Yeats, W.B., 107, 117
Ypres ['Wipers'],
  salient, 46, 50
  Third Battle of, 49

Index of references to Owen's poems